The Reverend Wm. T. Sprole D.D.

with the respects of

Chas. Johnston

October 17. 1856.

John Johnston

THE

AUTOBIOGRAPHY

AND

MINISTERIAL LIFE

OF

THE REV. JOHN JOHNSTON, D.D.

EDITED AND COMPILED BY

THE REV. JAMES CARNAHAN, D.D.,
LATE PRESIDENT OF THE COLLEGE OF NEW JERSEY.

Together with an Appendix.

NEW YORK:
M. W. DODD, 59 CHAMBERS STREET.

1856

R. CRAIGHEAD, PRINTER,
53 Vesey Street, New York.

PREFACE.

The late Rev. Dr. A. Alexander, a man full of good deeds, proposed at the Board of Trustees of the College of New Jersey, that a blank book be provided, and that a brief notice of Graduates of the College be recorded therein. This proposition was adopted, and the book was committed to the mover of the resolution, and he filled one hundred and ten large folio pages with notices of different Alumni of the College, chiefly from his own knowledge. After the decease of Dr. Alexander, this book was placed in the hands of the subscriber, with a request that the notices be continued.

With a view to prepare a brief account of the late Rev. John Johnston, D.D., a Graduate and Trustee of the College, an inspection of such papers as contained information touching the subject was asked and kindly granted by the family of the deceased.

On examination, these papers were found to contain some account of himself and of the churches with which he had been connected, written for the gratification of his friends. These documents exhibit the character of a good man, worthy in many respects of imitation, and also a fuller account of the origin and progress of a portion of the Presbyterian Church than is elsewhere to be found. The original design of recording a brief account of the individual was abandoned, and the papers were arranged, and are now printed, together with such information as came within the knowledge of the Editor. Such is the origin of the following work. It is right to state, that in noting some things respecting himself, Dr. Johnston had not the most remote idea that the narrative would be read in any other form than in his manuscript by his intimate friends. His modesty would have shrunk from the idea of exhibiting himself before the public as worthy of notice. Yet his biography is not less interesting and instructive because it was intended only for the gratification of his intimate friends. His long ministerial life is so interwoven with the history of the Presbyterian Church in the region between the cities of New York and Albany, that the one cannot be understood without a knowledge of the other. It is with a view of rescuing from oblivion important facts respecting that section of the Presbyterian Church, as well as of testifying our respect for the memory of a good and useful man, that we present this small book to the Christian reader, believing he will find in the perusal instruction and encouragement in the performance of his duty.

JAMES CARNAHAN.

CONTENTS.

CHAPTER I.

His parentage—His baptism—Early reminiscences—Dutch parsonage—Death of Colonel Barber—Small-pox—Removal to a farm—Going to school—The Bible read in school—Farming—Placed in a store—Conversation with his father respecting an occupation—Chooses an education—Commences Latin under his pastor, the Rev. J. Freeman—Advice given by his father—Goes to school in Montgomery—Removed to Kingston Academy—The death of his father—Makes arrangement to enter college—Drives cattle to market—Conversation of two little boys respecting God—Recognises one of these boys forty-five years afterwards......................9

CHAPTER II.

Journey to Princeton—No steamboats or railroads—The first steamboat—Enters college—The faculty—The want of class-books—His class-mates—College life—The state of religion in the college—Journey home in vacation—The death of General Washington—Anxiety after commencement—Thinks of the gospel ministry—Consults the Rev. A. King—Admitted to the communion of the church—Determines to prepare for the ministry—Returns to Princeton, to study under the direction of Dr. Smith—The burning of the college—Students scattered..................................25

CHAPTER III.

Determines to cross the mountains, and to study under the Rev. Dr. McMillan—Travels on horseback—Pennsylvania waggons—Mountain scenery—Goitre, and causes thereof—The country west of the mountains—The houses—Arrives at Canonsburg—Meets Dr. McMillan—His personal appearance—His preaching—Joins the theological class—Attends an ordination, in company with Dr. McMillan—Passes through Pittsburg—The course of study—An account of a remarkable revival of religion, attended with bodily affections..........37

CHAPTER IV.

Determines to return east of the mountains, to teach in a private family—An account of his journey—Passes through Baltimore and Annapolis—Crosses the Chesapeake—Finds the place engaged pre-occupied—Disappointment and great perplexity—Succeeds in obtaining another place—Incidents in Maryland—Leaves Maryland—Returns through Philadelphia to Orange county—Returns to Princeton, and studies under Dr. H. Kollock—Appointed tutor in the college—Incidents in that office—The Osage Indians...........................59

CHAPTER V.

Resigns tutorship—Licensed to preach—Returns to Orange county—Supplies vacant congregations, under the direction of the presbytery of Hudson—Accepts a call from the congregations of New Windsor and Newburgh—History of the church of New Windsor and

Newburgh—His marriage—His ordination—Commences housekeeping—Resigns thecharge of New Windsor, and gives his whole time to Newburgh—The origin of the church in Newburgh—The ministers who preceded him—The extent of his charge—An infidel club in Newburgh—Ignorance of the religious state of Newburgh—Opposition of friends to his location..................77

CHAPTER VI.

His first discourses after ordination—The way he treated infidelity, and the results—Pastoral duties during the first years of his ministry—Catechetical instruction, and Bible classes—Weekly lecture—Revivals in 1812–13, in 1815–16, in 1819–20, in 1824–25, in 1831—New measures—Division of the synod into old and new school—The effect on vital piety—Revival in 1843—The reasons why the number of church members did not increase—Dismissions to other churches given when asked..98

CHAPTER VII.

The means used to watch over the members of his church, and to keep himself acquainted with the state of his congregation—Emmonism—Change of views and practice in baptizing children and adults—Re-baptizing Roman Catholics—Efforts to educate young men for the gospel ministry—The Wills of Robert and Marion Hall, and Gilbert King, establishing the Ed and King Scholarship in the Theological Seminary of Princeton—Ministers' wives—Church music.....................129

CHAPTER VIII.

Efforts to organize a Second Presbyterian church in Newburgh—Extract of an address on that subject—The result—The Second church becomes New School, and is dissolved—The increase of churches in Newburgh—Improvement in morals—Drs. Brown and McCarroll—The extent of the original Presbytery of Hudson—Vacant congregations and supplies—Hudson Presbytery divided, and North River Presbytery formed—Bedford Presbytery formed from North River Presbytery—Two New School Presbyteries formed from these—Increase of ministers—Punctuality in attending Presbytery and other judicatories of the church—Fourteen times a Commissioner to the General Assembly—A delegate to the General Association of Connecticut and of Massachussets—A delegate to the General Association of New Hampshire and General Convention of Vermont—Biography of 140 ministers—Records of the Presbytery of Dutchess—Elected a Trustee of the College of New Jersey—The degree of Doctor in Divinity conferred 148

CHAPTER IX.

Review of his Ministry—Seven Discourses—His last illness—Noble Resolution of his Congregation—The Visit of Two Friends—Partial Recovery—Attends Commencement at Princeton—His Death—Funeral Services.......171

CHAPTER X.

Concluding Summary....................181

APPENDIX....................197

AUTOBIOGRAPHY.

CHAPTER I.

His parentage—His baptism—Early reminiscences—Dutch parsonage—Death of Colonel Barber—Small-pox—Removal to a farm—Going to school—The Bible read in school—Farming—Placed in a store—Conversation with his father respecting an occupation—Chooses an education—Commences Latin under his pastor, the Rev. J. Freeman—Advice given by his father—Goes to school in Montgomery—Removed to Kingston Academy—The death of his father—Makes arrangement to enter college—Drives cattle to market—Conversation of two little boys respecting God—Recognises one of these boys forty-five years afterwards.

To profit myself, and to gratify my friends, I have determined to note a few things respecting myself, from my birth to the present time.

My parents were from the north of Ireland.

My father from the county of Cavan, and my mother from Longford.

My father, the youngest of thirteen children, was often heard to say, that his great-grandfather came from England, in connexion with the army under King William, and fought in the battle of the Boyne, July 1st, 1690. When the army was disbanded he remained in Ireland, and settled in the county of Cavan. There my father was born, December 1st, 1743, his parents being in connexion with the Episcopal church. In 1774 he emigrated to this country, and located himself in the province of New York, intending to return to his native land at the end of seven years. In the year 1775 my mother, Jane Moncriff, in company with her brother Charles, arrived in this country, and tarried with a distant relative, in the neighborhood where my father resided. Although in the old country my father and mother had no knowledge of each other, their common origin on the Emerald Isle led to an acquaintance, which terminated in marriage in 1777.

On the 28th of January, 1778, I was born, in the township of Montgomery and county of Ulster, but now (1851) township of Crawford and county of Orange, State of New York. I was named John, the name of my paternal grandfather. My constitution appeared to be feeble, and it was thought by my parents and their neighbors that my days would probably be but few. My father's intention of returning to Ireland was frustrated by the revolutionary war, which commenced soon after his arrival in this country; and before the close of the war his marriage and family connexions were such as precluded the hope of returning to the home of his ancestors.

I have heard my parents say, that when the frame of the Presbyterian church in Hopewell was erecting I was laid on a blanket under the shade of a tree. This was probably in the summer of 1778. My father had a better education than many of the immigrants from Ireland, and he was employed nearly seven years in one neighborhood in teaching school. In the spring of 1779 my parents removed into the parsonage house of the Reformed Dutch church; and by a minister of that church I was baptized, although at that time neither my father nor my mother were members, in full communion, in any church. My father was educated in the Episcopal church, and my mother was brought up in connexion with the Presbyterian church in Ireland. She afterwards became a member, in full communion, in the Presbyterian church of Hopewell, and remained such until her death. My father was as actively engaged in the support of the Presbyterian church in Hopewell, as if he had been a member in full communion. He was one of the trustees, did whatever writing was necessary, and kept the accounts of the congregation.

I have a distinct recollection of several things which occurred during the revolutionary war. I remember the erection of liberty poles, and the death of Colonel Barber, a particular friend of my father. The colonel was killed by the falling of a tree, on Saturday, and the report of his death was brought on Sabbath morning, by persons coming to public worship. My father was greatly affected, and shed tears. This arrested my attention, and was so deeply impressed on my mind that I have at this day a distinct recollection of the event, although it occurred when I was not more than five years old.

At that time there was no little prejudice against inoculation, and the inhabitants of the neighborhood generally dreaded the spread of the small-pox. And as the parsonage was considered common property, it was resolved to make it a hospital, for the accommodation of all who thought proper to submit themselves, or the members of their families, to inoculation. Some forty or fifty persons, most of them children, came together and were packed away in one of the rooms, and the doctor and his attendants were in another. Then came the general performance. The patients came in singly, with a cloth saturated with whiskey applied to the nose, and with eyes turned away from the doctor held out the arm that had been made bare, and after a breathless silence of a minute or two the patient made way for another, and so on until the whole had undergone the inoculating process. I ought to have stated, that we had previously been together for a few days undergoing the preparatory process—living on mush without salt, and no meat of any kind. Medicine was given in abundance, and as it was administered in molasses it created in me such a disgust that I have loathed molasses ever since. The whole terminated favorably, and generally without leaving a pit or mark.

In the spring of 1783 our family removed from the Dutch parsonage to the western part of the town of Montgomery, now known as the town or township of Crawford. And although the distance was only three miles, the common remark was, that Master Johnston (so called as having been a school teacher) and his family had removed back into the woods. It was then an unsettled part of the town, and yet in about thirty-five years that same neighborhood in which my parents were the pioneers was considered the most highly cultivated part of the county. Four farmers in that neighborhood took the premium for five successive years for having the best cultivated farms in the county. The distance we lived from the school was more than two miles, and when I was scarce nine years old I, and a sister younger than myself, travelled that distance on foot, day after day, summer and winter. The principal book read in the school was the Bible, and I can to this day repeat with readiness passages which I then committed to memory; and I recollect, with precision, the history of the deluge, of Joseph, and Moses, and Sampson, and David, and Goliah, and others which arrested my attention. This single fact has convinced me of the importance of a careful and constant use of the Holy Scriptures in every system of common school education.

I was engaged on the farm as soon as I was able to work, and have reason to believe that the active life I was compelled to live strengthened my constitution, naturally feeble, and enabled me to estimate what might reasonably be expected from a laboring man when employed in my service, and also taught me how to use and take care of animals. I can remember days of labor and work performed which would now be thought unreasonable if exacted from a youth of similar age. I have many a day followed the plough from morning to night. I have oftentimes had to obtain assistance to relieve the plough fastened under a root or stone.'

In the fall of 1794 I went to remain for the winter in the store of a man who lived three miles distant. In the spring, when, on a Monday morning, I was preparing to return to the store, my father told me to sit down, that he wished to have a conversation with me; and he went on to say, that it was time I began to think what I would wish to be employed in for life; that he had been thinking, that if I preferred farming he would purchase a farm which was for sale, and it would be ready by the time I would want it; or, if I wished to be a merchant, I must complete my clerkship, and he would try to help me in commencing business; or, if I chose an education, I should have that. "Take time," said he, "to consider these propositions, and when you have made up your mind let me know, and my conduct shall be regulated accordingly. But remember, when you decide it must be a final decision; I will have no change."

I replied, "Father, I am ready."

He tried to dissuade me from an immediate decision. But I replied that I was as ready to decide now as I would ever be.

"And what," said he, "is your decision?"

I said, "Give me the books."

"Well," said he, "go and bring home your effects from the store, and you must remain with me on the farm until the fall harvest is gathered in, and then you shall have your discharge."

I did as directed; and I do not know that Jacob served his time more cheerfully, in view of obtaining Rachel, than I labored through the summer, in the prospect of obtaining an education.

On the 14th of December, 1795, I entered upon a course of study, under the direction of the Rev. Jonathan Freeman, pastor of the congregation of Hopewell. There were also three others, sons of farmers belonging to the pastoral charge of Mr. Freeman, who commenced study with myself. One of them is a wealthy farmer, still living; the other two are dead. One of them became a minister of the gospel, and, after thirty years of usefulness, died in the midst of his people, in the hope of a blessed immortality; the other, after spending much money to no valuable purpose, died in early life.

My father used to counsel me in reference to certain places and practices, which made a deep impression on my mind, and which has been of great service to me all my life. So impressed was I with his counsels, that I cannot to this day remain long in a tavern without feeling condemned. The old gentleman was a deadly enemy to theatres; and such was the effect of his admonitions on the subject, that I have never been inside of a theatre, or attended a public ball in my life. As to Free-masonry, he lived and died in the full belief that Free-masons had dealings with the devil; and erroneous as this opinion may have been, his counsels on the subject have had the effect of preventing me entering a lodge, and I am not conscious that I have ever had a desire to know what the mysteries of Masonry are. He was always ready to explain to children the reasons why he performed any act. I remember, when I was about ten years of age, asking him why he cut the upper end of a stake which he was going to drive into the ground, square or even, and he replied, that he might drive it into the ground with the poll of the axe. This simple act, and the reason assigned for doing it, suggested to me the importance of forethought, and of adopting means suited to accomplish an end in view. Truly we know not what the result of a single act, or a single word, may be. Parents and instructors should always be ready to explain to children the reasons of what they do. Beneficial impressions may be made when least expected.

In the spring of 1797 the Rev. Mr. Freeman was preparing to remove and take charge of the congregation of Bethlehem, fifteen or twenty miles distant, and it became necessary to seek another instructor. My father procured boarding for me in the village of Montgomery, about a mile from the academy under the direction of Mr. Reuben Neely. I returned to my father's house every Saturday afternoon, and back to the school, eight miles distant, on Monday morning. Here I remained for two years, until Mr. Neely relinquished the charge of the academy. I was removed to an academy in Kingston, under the direction of Mr. Timothy Smith, who afterwards was appointed Professor of Ancient Languages in Union College. I remained in Kingston until the last day of September, when about sundown two men came to take me home, informing me that my father had died suddenly the preceding night. I arrived in time to see his corpse before its removal, and then followed his remains to the burying-ground connected with the church of "Goodwill."

This was a solemn providence; not only in the loss of an intelligent, affectionate, and devoted parent, but as it presented an insuperable obstacle (in my apprehension) to the completion of my education. It produced a train of thought solemn and trying, and I was often led to inquire, "What shall I do—what is best to be done?" Various plans presented themselves, and no sooner were they considered than they were abandoned. While some schemes would promise self-advantage, the comfort and happiness of my mother, and the rest of the family, would be overlooked. After some days were spent in this sad state of mind, my mother suggested that it would be best for me to go to college, and she would endeavor to keep the family together, and provide for me the means of completing my education. The subject was considered and talked of for several days, and finally it was agreed that I should enter college. As money would be wanted, it was proposed to dispose of some of the stock that could be spared. In company with a neighbor, who was in the habit of driving cattle into the counties of Dutchess and Westchester, I became a drover. This was a new business, but I engaged in it with alacrity, inasmuch as the result was to be for my benefit. After crossing the river at Newburgh, we visited Fishkill and Philipstown, and on the second day passed below Yorktown in Westchester. As sales had been made of a sufficient number of cattle to furnish me with money enough for my immediate wants, it was thought advisable that I should return.

Leaving the drov[illegible]e rest of the company, I returned as far as Yorktown, and took lodgings for the night. This was the first time in my life that I felt myself to be in a lonely situation. I was far from friends, and knew not that there was any individual near me that had ever heard of me, or cared for me. With these feelings I retired to rest, and in the morning, about daylight, I was waked by two little boys, in a trundle-bed at the foot of the bed in which I was, talking about God—wondering if God could see them—could he see them in the dark? could he see them if they covered heads with the blanket? and similar questions. Their conversation arrested my attention, and left an impression which I have never forgotten, and which has frequently occurred to me during the whole of my life. In this connexion I would remark, that some forty-five years after the occasion above stated I was brought to recognise one of these little boys, in the following manner:—During the meeting of our synod, in the city of New York, I was invited, with some twenty others, ministers and ruling elders, to dine with the Rev. Dr. Potts. At table the conversation turned on what has frequently occurred, viz. that great events often arose from apparently trivial circumstances—that the course of a man's life ofttimes was determined by a word dropped in conversation, or by a contingency over which the individual has no control. Reference was made to incidents in the life of George Whitefield, Dr. Rogers, Dr. McWhorter, and others. I was reminded of what occurred to myself at Yorktown, and I repeated the conversation of the two little boys, above stated, and remarked that that incident determined the course of my future life, and was the cause, under God, of my becoming a minister of the gospel, and a member of the synod of New York. A gentleman at the foot of the table inquired when, and where, and at whose house, that which I had related occurred. I answered, it was in the month of October, 1799, in Yorktown, at the house of Mr. Purdy, opposite the Presbyterian church. The gentleman, with quivering lips, and tears in his eyes, said, "I am one of those two little boys, and am here as a ruling elder in the Presbyterian church." "*Whoso is wise, and will observe these things, even they shall understand the loving kindness of the Lord.*"

I returned in safety to my mother's house, and in a few days began to prepare to visit Princeton. I ought here to remark, that I was the oldest of five children, and it might reasonably have been expected that I would have remained at home to take charge of the family; but my dear mother was willing to submit to all the toil and care of supporting the family, and of providing for me while pursuing my studies in the college.

CHAPTER II.

Journey to Princeton—No steamboats or railroads—The first steamboat—Enters college—The faculty—The want of class-books—His class-mates—College life—The state of religion in the college—Journey home in vacation—The death of General Washington—Anxiety after commencement—Thinks of the gospel ministry—Consults the Rev. A. King—Admitted to the communion of the church—Determines to prepare for the ministry—Returns to Princeton, to study under the direction of Dr. Smith—The burning of the college—Students scattered.

In the latter part of October, 1799, before daylight, I left my mother's house, about twenty miles west of Newburgh, and I did not reach Princeton until the next Saturday week, progressing as fast as the public conveyances would carry us. The easiest and most expeditious way was on board of a sloop, and two days and two nights in reaching New York was considered a good passage; and four or five days, and even more, as in my case, was not uncommon. From New York to Princeton the journey by stage was equally tedious.

In the fall of 1807 the first steamboat came up the river—the wheels unprotected, and exposed to public view. A form on cross beams, like that of a saw-mill, moving up and down, and the boat creeping along at the rate of three or four miles an hour. A real curiosity! the wonder of the country! People would come twenty or thirty miles, to see the boat on the day she was to make her trip. Then came an improved boat, such as would accommodate passengers, but it was a very different thing from the floating palaces in which we may now go at the rate of fifteen or twenty miles an hour, with lodging and fare equal to the best city hotels. There was no landing at the dock; the boat lay in the river, and we had to be rowed out in a small boat. I have been dragged in one of these row-boats until we were opposite New Windsor, in a dark night, before I ascended the steamer, and then could find no convenient place to sit, or stand, or lie; perhaps it was raining; nothing to eat, and I was glad to be let off at New York, after paying three and a half dollars for the passage. Railroads now extend in all directions. And on the east side of the Hudson you may go under mountains, through water, along the crooked margin of the river, with a rapidity outstripping the speed of the racehorse, moved by the old black horse that never tires. A trip to Princeton may now be made in half the number of hours that I was days on the way in my first visit, at less than half the expense!

After arriving at Princeton I was admitted to the Junior Class. The Faculty consisted of the Rev. Dr. Samuel Stanhope Smith, Dr. John McLean—father of the Rev. Dr. John Maclean—Henry Kollock and Frederic Beasley. The whole number of students was not more than seventy-five or eighty, and even all these were not in full standing. It was at that time the custom to permit students not acquainted with Latin or Greek, especially Greek, to attend to English and scientific studies with the regular students, and at the end of their course to give them a certificate, and not a regular diploma, specifying the studies to which they had attended. Hence the classes at that period in the triennial catalogue are small, not containing more than two-thirds, and in some cases one half of those in actual attendance. Text books at that time were not so easily obtained as they are now. Dr. Smith's lectures on Moral Philosophy, which were voluminous, had to be copied; and also a syllabus of Dr. Maclean's Lectures on Chemistry. Neither my room-mate nor myself could obtain in New York or Philadelphia a copy of Simpson's Algebra, the text book used. We adopted the plan of borrowing a book the day before that study was required, and when the day for algebra came, we were prepared. The consequence was that we were offered books by the lazy part of the class, who, in return for the use of their books, received from us instruction without the labor of study. Teaching others, made us so familiar with the subject, that at the close of the term, or year, we had the honor of being named among the best scholars in the class, so far as algebra was concerned.

Among my class-mates were several individuals who became distinguished and useful men in after life, such as Nicholas Biddle of Philadelphia, Dr. John E. Cook of Virginia, since Professor of the Theory and Practice of Medicine in the University of Transylvania, Ky.; the Rev. Dr. John McDowell, now of Philadelphia, Henry E. Watkins, Edward D. Watts, and John G. Gamble of Virginia.

I became a member of the American Whig Society in the College, and I felt an interest and zeal in its honor and prosperity, which the lapse of half a century has not extinguished.

Having been accustomed all my previous life to mingle freely with the society of male and female, and to enjoy the sociality of the domestic circle, I found it rather tough, especially during the first term of nearly six months, to be excluded from those I loved, and to confine my attention to angles and triangles, and algebraic surds and equations. We had monthly holidays, and I found some relief from the monotony of college life, in visiting on these occasions the family of Andrew McDowell, a relative of my room-mate, who resided about nine miles from the college.

The sociability of that agreeable and hospitable family restored in some measure the elasticity of my spirits, and caused me to anticipate the pleasure I should enjoy on returning in the approaching vacation to the social circle of my early days.

The state of religion was lamentably low in the college. Among the students there were only three or four who made any pretensions to piety. The only means of grace enjoyed the first session was morning and evening prayers in the chapel, a sermon in the forenoon on the Sabbath, and prayer meeting in the evening of the same day, at which none except the tutors and three or four students attended. I usually attended, but took no active part in conducting the services, which consisted in prayer and reading a sermon, for none who attended were skilled in music or were able to sing. The following summer term or session of the college, Mr. H. Kollock, who still remained a tutor, was licensed to preach, and he usually occupied the pulpit in the village church on the Sabbath afternoons. So eloquent and popular was he, that nearly all the students voluntarily attended, and many persons from neighboring congregations came, and the house was crowded with attentive hearers.

At the close of my first college term, in company with three other students, I hastened to the public-house to wait the arrival of the mail stage for New York. When it arrived, there were in it four sailors, just landed from a distant voyage. The rule was that not more than six passengers could have a seat within the stage unless with the consent of those already in. Two of the students immediately rushed into the stage. I was one of two without a seat. We begged to be admitted; the driver said "no!" except with the unanimous consent of those occupying the seats. At last Jack cried out to me, "come in, my hammock will hold us both." The other student took a seat with the coachman on the box, and we were soon on our way. The roads were in a sad state. The stage was often so sunk in the mud, that four horses could not extricate it, and we were under the necessity, as Jack said, of going "on shore." "The craft had grounded." It appeared to me that every sea term used by every sailor throughout the length and breadth of the land and ocean was in constant use. One of the sailors lost his hat *overboard,* and when we came to Newark, he *landed,* and pounded at the door of a hatter, until he was supplied.

On another occasion, returning home, we took sloop at New Brunswick, and when we reached Amboy, the tide and wind were against us, and it was proposed to have a supper of oysters. And although I had often tried, I had heretofore failed to eat oysters; but as my companions were going to have an oyster supper, I concluded to go with them. I ordered what I thought to be sufficient for myself to be shucked and fried. These were brought forward first, and in a minute or two they were all gone. Then came the roasted; and as I saw my shipmates eating heartily, I thought it was too bad to pay fifty cents for a single cup of coffee: "I'll try and eat two or three little ones." I did so; and I continued until I had as large a pile of shells as any one at the table. Thus *commenced* my fondness for oysters, and it has continued to the present time.

Shortly after I entered college, the public learned the melancholy fact, that on the 14th day of December, 1799, General Washington died, at his residence on the banks of the Potomac. At the request of citizens of Trenton, Dr. Smith, president of the college, consented to deliver, on the 14th of January, 1800, in the city of Trenton, an oration, commemorative of the virtues and services of that great and good man. On the day appointed a large number of the students, the greater part on foot, repaired to Trenton. So great was the throng, that the students and many others had to stand on their feet. After the eulogy, which Dr. Smith delivered in his most elegant and impressive manner, the military proceeded to inter a coffin, according to the honors of war; Governor Howell, who had been with Washington in the battle of Monmouth, following the hearse as chief mourner. When the ceremonies were closed, we made our way back to the college. To walk ten miles going and ten miles returning, and to stand on our feet nearly three hours, was not a small day's labor. It will be believed, that when we reached the college we were excessively fatigued and hungry, for we had no opportunity to get anything to eat during the day.

I have frequently seated myself under the tree, and, after it was cut down, on the stump, where General Mercer was reported to lie mortally wounded, at the battle of Princeton. I have also gazed, with wet eyes, at the painting suspended in the college chapel, which represents a surgeon bending over Mercer expiring, and Washington, full size, standing near, with drawn sword.

When I told my father that I wished to have an education, I had no particular occupation or profession in view; but when I drew near to the close of my college course I became extremely anxious. I could not endure the idea of law or medicine. I felt that I had not the piety which I deemed indispensable in a minister of the gospel. From the time I had heard the two little boys talk about God seeing them in the dark, and covered with a blanket, I had serious reflections; but the gayeties and follies of the world soon caused them to pass away. As the time of commencement drew near my serious thoughts became more deep and lasting. On my way home I felt miserable, as the time had now come when I must decide as to my future course. When I thought of anything but the ministry I was wretched. When I thought of that a calm state of mind ensued. The subject was constantly before my mind, either in prayer or meditation. And the more I thought of the gospel ministry the more my thoughts were drawn towards it, and I hope at last with a fixed purpose to direct my studies towards a work in which I might glorify God and benefit my fellow men. I asked the advice of the Rev. Andrew King. And, after several interviews, I was admitted a member of the church of Goodwill, in the fall of 1801, a few weeks after I had received the degree of Bachelor of Arts.

My mind became settled, and I returned to Princeton to study divinity, under Dr. Smith. He prescribed a course of study; but I do not recollect that I ever recited to him on any branch of study. On the 6th of March following (1802) the college building was burned, the library destroyed, and the theological students scattered.

CHAPTER III.

Determines to cross the mountains, and to study under the Rev. Dr. McMillan—Travels on horseback—Pennsylvania waggons—Mountain scenery—Goitre, and causes thereof—The country west of the mountains—The houses—Arrives at Canonsburg—Meets Dr. McMillan—His personal appearance—His preaching—Joins the theological class—Attends an ordination, in company with Dr. McMillan—Passes through Pittsburg—The course of study—An account of a remarkable revival of religion, attended with bodily affections.

It then became a serious inquiry, what I should do. I had read and heard much of revivals of religion, but I had never witnessed one. As Dr. McMillan, in the western part of Pennsylvania, was spoken of as a minister whose labors had been blessed with several revivals, and as he was also an instructor in theology, I resolved to cross the mountains, and to prosecute my studies under his direction. I returned to my mother's house, in order to prepare to go to the waters of the Ohio. In April, 1802, I set out on my journey. My wardrobe was the saddle-bags on which I rode. My horse was not the finest in appearance, but sufficiently able to carry me over the Alleghany mountains. I took Princeton on my way, and having taken leave of my friends, I passed through Philadelphia, Lancaster, Columbia, and Yorktown, and rested on the Sabbath at Chambersburg. On Monday I proceeded on my journey, and passed through McConnell's Town, Bedford, and Somerset, crossing mountains and some *small* hills, one of which (Laurel hill) was only nine miles from foot to foot. On my journey, the large Pennsylvania waggons which I every day saw arrested my attention. They were of great size, and drawn by from four to eight horses, much larger than any I had ever seen. Sometimes they were harnessed two and two abreast, sometimes they were strung along single, one after the other. The leader walked majestically, with head reined up, as if he had nothing to do except to guide the procession. The shaft horse was content with holding back when going down hill, and then all his energies were called into action. The greater part of the commerce of western Pennsylvania, western Virginia, Ohio, and Kentucky, was carried on by means of these large waggons. They moved at the average rate of twelve miles each day, so that they were about three weeks making a trip from Philadelphia to Pittsburgh. The drivers were generally of the roughest class; their home was on the road summer and winter. They knew no Sabbath, lodging in their waggons in summer, and on the bar-room floor in winter. They were civil, and even obliging, to other travellers, if not molested, but showed themselves lords of the road if their rights were infringed. Woe be to the man in a light carriage who ordered them to give the road in a narrow pass in the mountains!

As I passed the mountains, the wildness and grandeur, and sometimes the beauty, of the scenery arrested my attention. Especially at the rising and setting of the sun, the prospect was sublime and glorious. The brilliant rays of the morning and evening sun, reflected from immense rocks on the summits of the mountains, the dark shades of the pines where his beams had not reached, and the fogs resting on the valleys, giving them the appearance of lakes and rivers, with rocks and leafless trees here and there projecting, was a panorama which filled my soul with wonder and amazement, and caused me to exclaim, "Great and marvellous are thy works, Lord God Almighty, in wisdom thou hast made them all!"

The prospect, in looking back from the summit of the first mountain west of Chambersburg, presenting to view the great fertile valley which extends through Pennsylvania, Maryland, and Virginia, was beautiful and enchanting. Nor was that from the west side of the same mountain, which overlooks the extensive plain on which McConnell's Town is situated, less so. The wild and precipitous descent to the Juniata, and the immense piles of rock, on which a shrub can scarcely find a foothold, near Bedford, are still, after a lapse of half a century, vividly before my mind.

On the summit of the Alleghany Mountains, I

lodged at the sign of the Whitehorse, and I was kept awake part of the night lest I should be robbed of what little cash I had by a fellow who slept in the same room with me. Perhaps my fears were groundless. Rough-looking men are not always rogues, nor are smooth-looking men always honest. At the foot of the Laurel Hill, where I had stopped to feed my horse, a woman, with an uncommonly long neck, came into the room in which I was, and she had a frightfully large tumor in front of her throat; and she breathed with so much difficulty that I feared she would fall down suffocated. This was the first case I had ever seen of the goitre. But I found that disease was very common west of the mountains. In Switzerland it is accounted for, from the water used for drink being melted snow. In western Pennsylvania, some suppose the cause to be the use of water filtering through the strata of bituminous coal that underlies the face of the country. Other causes are assigned, such as the decomposition of vegetable matter in connexion with the coal formation in the country. Others, again, think it arises from the want of salted marine-fish, and remark that this malady is usually found in regions remote from the seaboard; and that fish-skins applied to the throat, externally, is one of the best remedies; and the theory is favored by the fact that this disease is much less frequent since the means of conveyance have so improved, that salted fish are carried beyond the mountains.

The face of the country west of the mountains is very uneven; the hills do not run in parallel ranges, but, like a seal-skin, the risings and depressions are without any order. The land is fertile, with very few stones or rocks visible on the surface. Wheat, rye, and grass grow luxuriantly on the top and sides of hills, so steep, that the plough is used with difficulty. The whole country seems to be bedded with bituminous coal. So plenty was that article, that we had it laid at our door, ready for use, for two and a half cents a bushel.

The houses in the mountains built for the accommodation of travellers, and, indeed, many on farms and in villages west of the mountains, were constructed of logs, notched together at the corners, and the chinks between filled with billets of wood, and mortar made of clay.

I arrived, about the last of May, at Canonsburg, situated twenty miles south of Pittsburg, and seven miles north of Washington, the capital of the county of the same name. Jefferson College, located there, was then in its infancy, with John Watson, whose history is full of interest, at its head. As I drew near to the village, I met a large country-looking man with a little stoop in his broad shoulders, a long nose and long neck, and head projecting forward more than usual, and in his hand he had an uncommonly large walking-stick. From the description I had heard of him, I concluded it was the Apostle of the West; but I could not command confidence enough to speak to him. The next day, when he rose in the pulpit to commence public worship, I perceived that my conjectures were well founded. It was the veritable John McMillan. I heard him preach with no little attention; and the opinion I then, and afterwards, formed, I believe to be correct, that he analysed and brought to light the secret workings of the deceitful human heart, beyond any man I ever heard preach. His preaching was with power, and he had many souls as seals of his ministry, and crowns of rejoicing in the day of the Lord Jesus. Mr. Andrew Thompson, who had been my class-mate from the commencement of my classical studies until we finished our college course, on being informed of my arrival, was soon with me, and conducted me to the house of Mrs. Whiteside, with whom I boarded about a year. Mr. Thompson had gone to Canonsburg six months before me—having set out for the West soon after commencement—I was soon introduced to Father McMillan and his family.

The first Sabbath I attended public worship I was forcibly struck with the multitude of voices engaged in singing. If a stranger did not sing, he was noticed and spoken of as the man who did not sing. And although the music was not of the most correct and scientific kind, it was hearty, impressive, and devout, and had a most thrilling and solemn effect, especially when the worship was in the open air, under the shade of the native trees, as was usually the case in the summer season. I could not but feel that God was among the people with his gracious presence. I took my place in the theological class, and, as nearly as I can recollect, I was the twenty-seventh person who had studied theology under Dr. McMillan. He had a manuscript system of questions and answers, of which we could have a copy if we would take the labor of transcribing. The system was plain and didactic rather than polemic. It was modelled after the plan of the old Puritan divines, particularly Flavel and Boston, and those of a kindred character and spirit. Very little attention was paid to the languages in which the sacred Scriptures were originally written, or to church history after the coming of Christ; Biblical history, the sacraments, and didactic theology, were the principal studies. There were seven or eight in the class, who in turn read or delivered discourses. To tell the truth, there was very little study, especially after the month of September. About four weeks after I commenced study, I went with Dr. McMillan to attend an ordination, west of the Alleghany river, above Pittsburg. When we reached the top of the immense hill overlooking Pittsburg, and south of the Monongahela, I was amazed at the sight of the beautiful plain lying far below us, on which Pittsburg is situated. It was not then, as now, covered with dwelling-houses, and factories of various kinds, and overshadowed with a dense cloud of smoke, sent from the coal used to impel the machinery. We could see the clear blue water of the Alleghany coming from the north-east, and the turbid waters of the Monongahela coming from the south, meeting each other at the point where once stood Fort Duquesne, forming the beautiful Ohio, flowing towards the south-west between the surrounding hills. Little did I think, when enjoying the delightful prospect, that I was standing on an immense strata of bituminous coal; and perhaps there were miners at that moment beneath my feet, using the pick and shovel.

We lodged in Pittsburg, and the following day crossed the Alleghany about four miles above, and then went seven or eight miles into the woods, attended the ordination and returned to

Pittsburg. By appointment previously made, Dr. McMillan preached in the evening one of his thundering sermons, calculated to alarm impenitent sinners. A very large part of our time as students was spent in complying with a practice which prevailed in that part of the country. The Lord's Supper was administered only twice a year in each congregation; but the custom was for three or four churches to come together on these occasions. Thursday was a fast day—in some places there was preaching on Friday—on Saturday there were two public services, and prayer meetings in the evening. On the Sabbath the services were often continued from ten o'clock in the morning until near sunset, and then prayer meetings at private houses in the evening. On Monday there was preaching in the morning, and sometimes in the afternoon. Theological students were expected to attend these sacramental occasions, far and near. So great was the concourse, that sometimes the men had to lodge in a barn or hay-mow. I have often attended a hay-mow prayer meeting in the dark. A hymn would be repeated from memory and sung, a prayer offered, and singing and prayer would be repeated several times, or religious conversation or exhortation would take place. I have attended several sacramental seasons at the distance of seven, fifteen, and one twenty-seven miles, and generally on foot. At this time I can call to mind the impressive and solemn exercises of mind which I had on these occasions. Returning from one of these blessed seasons, I distinctly remember retiring into the woods, and by the side of a fallen tree, I had such a view of my sinfulness, especially the depravity of my heart, as exceeded anything I had ever experienced before, and which caused the way of salvation through the atonement of the Lord Jesus Christ to be precious, and the only way in which I desired salvation. At the remembrance thereof, I can use the language of Job, and say: "oh, that it were with me as in days that are past."

In October, 1802, the Synod of the same name met in Pittsburg. My room-mate, who had been there, returned on Friday evening, and gave an account of a revival of religion which had commenced in the congregations of the Rev.

Elisha McCurdy. The subjects in the beginning of the awakening were generally exercised with great bodily agitations. There was no one characteristic mark of this bodily exercise. Sometimes it would so affect the person, that a stranger, ignorant of the cause, would be ready to conclude that the person affected, had epilepsy, or was dying. Sometimes convulsions were so violent that it would require two or three persons not affected, to prevent injury. Sometimes a cramp would pervade the whole body, and an attempt to part the fingers would require considerable effort, and when the force applied was suddenly suspended, the fingers would return to their original position, like a bent bow, when relieved from the force which drew it aside from its natural position. Some would remain for hours in an apparent state of insensibility, and yet, when relieved, they could mention the prayers that had been made, the hymns that had been sung, or the sermon that had been delivered, while they were in this apparent stupor. Sometimes the same person would fall again and again for several months, others would have only a single fall.

In one instance, a minister fell in his pulpit, and in another, an elder, while distributing the elements on a sacramental occasion. Sometimes the stoutest and hardiest men would be seized, while the weak and feeble of their own families would be exempt. Sometimes those affected, would say, after they recovered, that they were not conscious of any mental excitement at the time they became powerless. The general declaration was, that their minds were agitated in view of their own guilt, or by sympathy with those around them. Sometimes a person would be taken when entirely alone and without being able to assign any cause. The greater part, however, became affected under religious feeling, when alone, or in their family, or in prayer meeting, or in the house of God. Sometimes the appearance would indicate to a spectator, that bodily affection was about to take place. Sometimes it would occur suddenly, when the countenance appeared calm and unmoved. Sometimes it was evident that sympathy was the exciting cause. A word or two would be followed by bodily affection in a single instance, and then another and another, until standing in a common sized room, I could touch with my cane at least one dozen prostrate on the floor at the same time—and perhaps no two of them affected in the same way—some praying, some silent, and others crying out in tones approaching shrieking. Some would remain a shorter and some a longer time in this state.

Sometimes those who had been frequently seized with bodily convulsions, would free themselves from mental distress, and their bodily affections would leave them, and they would become worse than they had ever been—scoffers at religion—ridiculers of those, who like themselves had been fools enough to suffer themselves to be wrought on in this ridiculous way. Many were bodily affected who never obtained a hope of an interest in Christ; and many, during this wonderful excitement, obtained a good hope who never were bodily affected. The same kind of bodily agitation extended through all the congregations belonging to the Presbytery of Ohio, and as nearly as I can recollect, thirteen or fourteen hundred were added to the communion of the churches. Many of the subjects of this extraordinary religious excitement have become faithful and useful preachers of the gospel. Though there were several things connected with that revival which I did not then, nor do I now understand, nor do I think essential to true religion, I have no more doubt that it was a genuine revival than I have that I am now writing with a pen made of a goose-quill. I verily believe that the proportion of those bodily affected, and who gave evidence of a change of heart, will not suffer in comparison with those only mentally affected in ordinary revivals of religion. God, for wise purposes, saw fit to permit this bodily affection (in which there was no piety) to accompany the saving influences of the Holy Spirit. Ministers were very careful in their preaching to distinguish between what were, and what were not, the gracious operations of the Holy Ghost.

One thing which then caused me much thought, and which was the subject of conversation with many of us, was the apparent coldness of ministers and good old elders, who had been praying for years for this blessed outpouring of the Holy Spirit. I well recollect that these were our thoughts respecting Drs. McMillan and Ralston, and Mr. Marquis and others, whose praise is in all the churches. Had not these men been cautious, and rather checked than added fuel to the heat of the day, there would have been a flame that would have scorched, if not burned up the church in that region. From President Edwards's narrative, and other sources, we learn that there were similar bodily affections in New England, Cambuslang in Scotland, and elsewhere, a hundred years ago. Ministers in Western Pensylvannia were aware of these facts, and were not surprised at these extraordinary manifestations, and they did not abstain in public and in private, from teaching that there was no genuine piety in bodily exercises.

I never was bodily affected during the whole of the revivals, although I was actively engaged in conducting religious worship in several congregations. It was agreed to have a general meeting, to be continued several days, including the Sabbath following. I was present. From twelve to fifteen ministers attended, and the number of communicants on the Lord's Day was more than one thousand—a large number, considering the sparseness of the population. Two weeks after this, there was another general meeting, and then, all the theological students went to be actively engaged in carrying on the work of the Lord. These were pentecostal seasons, in which many were pricked to the heart and hopefully brought to embrace the Lord Jesus as their Saviour. Yet there were those who were ready to say: "these men, if not full of new wine," are beside themselves; and among them were professors of religion, and even ministers of the gospel. Days of fasting and prayer were held, to beseech God that they might not fall into the fatal delusion which possessed the people.

I distinctly recollect several cases of remarkable conversions, one or two of which I will mention: Dr. Hare, a man of strong mind, and of an uncommonly athletic frame of body—I think he had been a surgeon in the Revolutionary army—had been exposed to great danger and had witnessed many scenes of blood and carnage. He had been sceptical, and professed to be an atheist—and yet even this man was prostrated on a Sabbath evening. A minister, an old acquaintance, spoke to him, reminding him of his dependence on God, urging him to obey God and accept the salvation of the gospel. He raised himself up, and said: "There is a God! I feel there is a God; but to me he is an angry God." The early part of the evening he attended public and social worship. When the congregation came together on Monday, the Doctor was missing, and from the agony in which he was on the preceding evening, it was feared he had chosen strangling rather than life. But he came out of the woods, where he had been praying, and took his seat in the congregation. He left the place in great distress, and several weeks elapsed before he found peace in believing. I saw him on several sacramental occasions afterwards, and his custom was to speak to the young people, and to sing and pray with them. By his life and conversation he gave practical evidence to his dying day, which occurred several years after, that he was a new creature in Christ Jesus.

Another remarkable case occurs to my mind. It is that of an old waggoner's wife. She was a woman of notoriously bad character—apparently as far from the kingdom of God as any one could be—she was greatly affected, and she was generally avoided on account of her known infamous character. Mrs. McMillan, the wife of Dr. McMillan, and myself, went and supported her when she was not able to support herself. She was very ignorant as well as wicked. We presented to her the simple truths of the gospel, telling her that Jesus Christ came into the world to save sinners, and that he could save to the uttermost, all who came to God through him, even the chief of sinners. She fell again and again, and did not find peace to her soul for many months after I left the country. While men and women avoided her, the Holy Spirit was striving with her, and she became hopefully pious, as I have learned, by letters, and manifested a change of heart by a life of holy obedience, until her death, which occurred several years afterwards.

It is not to be thought that only the ignorant

and profane were subject to bodily exercises. Some of the most moral and exemplary, and even some, whose piety, before and after, was unquestioned, were unable to control their muscular powers.

The image of good old James Edgar, an elder in the Presbyterian church, as he sat on a flatted log for a seat, holding an interesting little girl on his arm, praying and dropping a tear on her face, is still vividly before me. When she rose up, and spoke of Jesus as her precious savior, the old gentleman remarked with tears in his eyes, that God had honored his arms as the birthplace of one of his children. This Mr. Edgar was a remarkable man for intelligence, prudence, and exemplary piety. For many years he was one of the Associate Judges in the County of Washington; had frequently represented his district in the Legislature, and had been a member of the convention which formed the constitution of Pennsylvania. He also had great influence in restraining the violence of the people, and in quelling the insurrection of 1794, in the western counties. During this revival, I must have visited not less than ten or twelve congregations, and I was made acquainted with the ministers who conducted it; and a more pious, devoted and self-denying set of men I never knew. Their preaching had much to do with the heart, the temptations of the devil, the helplessness of the sinner, the necessity of a change of heart by the power of the Holy Spirit, of immediately ceasing to fight against God, of believing in Christ, whose righteousness alone was adequate to the demands of the divine law.*

* See Appendix A.

CHAPTER IV.

Determines to return east of the mountains, to teach in a private family—An account of his journey—Passes through Baltimore and Annapolis—Crosses the Chesapeake—Finds the place engaged pre-occupied—Disappointment and great perplexity—Succeeds in obtaining another place—Incidents in Maryland—Leaves Maryland—Returns through Philadelphia to Orange county—Returns to Princeton, and studies under Dr. H. Kollock—Appointed tutor in the college—Incidents in that office—The Osage Indians.

IN the summer of 1803 I was taken under the care of the Presbytery of Ohio, as a candidate for the gospel ministry. And I was strongly urged to take license, and to engage in the work of a missionary. This I could not conscientiously do. And as my means of support were nearly exhausted I determined to suspend study for some time, and to engage in teaching. I wrote to a friend on the subject, laid my plan before him, and he loaned me one hundred dollars, to enable me to pay my debts, and to return to the east side of the mountains. My plan was opposed by good old Dr. McMillan. He went so far as to say, it was a temptation of the devil, and that if I persisted in attempting to flee from my duty the hand of the Lord would arrest me, as it did Jonah in a similar case; and hereafter, although I might be saved as by fire, I would suffer loss. And although his warning caused me many serious thoughts, and no little prayer, I felt constrained to do as I had proposed. When it was known that I would go, a prayer-meeting was held at Dr. McMillan's house, where I boarded, and with much feeling I was commended to the care and keeping of Almighty God.

About the 1st of December, 1803, I took my leave of that region of country, endeared to me by many considerations. There I hope I learned more of myself and of my Saviour than I had ever known before; there I had become acquainted with many with whom I hope to be associated in another and a better world; there I left behind me those who would not cease to pray for me; and there, I verily believe, were many of God's dear children with whom I had taken sweet counsel, and gone up to the courts of the Lord's house. My heart was full, and my eyes overflowed, as I turned away from them, and set out, solitary and alone, to travel about four hundred miles, and to reside among strangers. My old saddle-bag again became my wardrobe, and, mounted on a small, iron-grey, young mare, spirited, tough, and ready to contend for her rights, I directed my course to the mountains. The first night I lodged at the same house with two gentlemen who were to travel about two hundred miles the same road with myself. But in the morning they proceeded at such a rate that I could not consistently follow, remembering that "a righteous man regardeth the life of his beast." But before night they found that they had travelled too fast, especially at the commencement of a long journey, and I overtook them, and we proceeded together for several days.

In recrossing the mountains I noticed considerable improvement in the accommodations since I had passed them; but still not so good as they are at the present time. You had to see that your horse received what you ordered, and what you paid for. My mare was ever ready to take care of herself when she had a chance, and see that her rights were not invaded with impunity. On one occasion, oats were placed before her in a trough before the door. I remarked to the landlord that he had better cause his fowls to be driven away, or they might be injured. He laughed, and said he would risk the fowls if I would risk the oats. These remarks were scarcely made when my filly snapped at a rooster in the manger, retaining the head in her mouth, and causing the body to fly several feet. I paid for the oats, and left "mine host" and his headless rooster.

On the east side of the mountains I parted with my fellow travellers. They directed their course towards Philadelphia, and I towards Baltimore. I had made arrangements to teach in a gentleman's family on the eastern shore of Maryland. I lodged one night in Baltimore, and as I sat part of the evening in the public parlor I heard some men, who from their dress might have passed for gentlemen (one of them was sheriff of the county), conversing respecting scenes which had been acted in the city, and in which they had been engaged, that filled me with horror, and I felt as if I was called on to flee out of that city, lest the wrath of God should be poured upon me and all that dwelt therein.

I passed through Annapolis, crossed the Chesapeake Bay, and was landed on Kent Island. I remember that my feelings were interested for a poor black man who ferried me over a small branch that separates the island from the eastern shore. I lodged at Easton, and when I arrived at the house of the gentleman with whom I expected to reside, I found a young man from New England already engaged as a teacher. I had delayed beyond the time appointed, and the services of another who offered had been secured. I was directed to another gentleman who wanted a teacher in his family, and I called to see him, and I found that he had made arrangements with a young man from Yale College. Thus disappointed I returned to the house of the gentleman in whose family I had expected to be employed, and remained for the night. The next day was the Sabbath, and it rained excessively. On Monday, after breakfast, I proceeded towards the State of New York, taking Easton in my way, near which place the second gentleman resided in whose family I had applied to be employed. The rain fell in torrents, and I was engaged in thinking on my unpleasant situation; I had borrowed one hundred dollars, and had no prospect of employment. I was miserable, and, I may say, almost desperate. I saw no way of repaying the money which I had borrowed. And as I rode along I came to the conclusion, that I would go to Baltimore, sell my horse, saddle, and bridle, and ship myself on board the first vessel leaving the port, whether for the east, west, north, or south. This idea was dwelt on for some time, as a relief from the uncertainty before me. But the thought occurred to my mind, What will ——, the young lady to whom I was engaged to be married, think?* My

* Thus God, in his adorable providence, makes use of

plans were arrested, and my tears flowed, and I scarcely knew what I thought or what I did. I came to the house of my friend, and determined to remain with him for the night, and in the morning to proceed towards the State of New York, not knowing what I would do, or what would become of me.

After the ladies had retired in the evening and the gentleman and myself were left alone in the parlor—"Out of the abundance of the heart the mouth speaketh"—I was led to give a short history of myself, and in return he also gave me a short history of himself. He also had had trials and sorrows. We found ourselves in tears and so retired to bed. In the morning I prepared to go on my way, and after breakfast ordered my horse. He said, "that I must not go yet." I remained an hour or more, and again ordered my horse. He replied, "he had concluded to employ me in his family, and that I must stay with him." This was unexpected, and I objected, saying that the young man in Connecticut ex-

natural affection to restrain from evil his erring children, when a sense of duty is too feeble.—Ed.

pected to come, and I did not wish any human being subjected to the same feelings I had experienced by disappointment. "But," said he, "you must stay; I have made up my mind, if he comes, to pay his expenses coming and returning, and you must stay." I did so, and I remained in his family a year and a half. There I became acquainted with some of the leading men in the State, the Tilghmans and Lloyds, Goldsboroughs, Smiths and others.

With Mr. Henry Nichols I remained until May, 1805, at a salary of three hundred dollars a year, with boarding and washing and my horse kept. I had the charge of his children, and the children of his sister, who had been married to a Mr. DeComsey. A son of Dr. More and daughter of Lawyer Buttel, were also my pupils; likewise the son of Thomas Hayward, whose father had been Attorney-General of the State of Maryland. I endeavored to teach them, not only to become acquainted with human science, but to know him whom to know aright is life eternal.

Mr. Nichols, the gentleman with whom I lived, was an episcopalian, and with him and his family I attended the episcopal church during my residence in Maryland. Our family was intimate with the Goldsboroughs, the Tilghmans, the Kerrs, the Chamberlains, the Lloyds, the Nelsons and others. On one occasion I went with the family to a dining party; I saw high life indeed, and it was the only time that I attended. The families of the Nichols and the Haywards were in the habit of visiting each other on Saturdays, and then the blacks would draw the seine, and the ladies with their maids would cook the fish, crabs, lobsters, oysters, crocus, yellow perch, and once in a while a sheepshead.

It was the practice of the gentlemen to loosen the seine if it became entangled on a stone or root in the bottom of the bay. When the tide was low in the Chesapeake, the gentlemen who wished to amuse themselves, would each mount a horse, with spear in hand, and watch the motion of the rock-fish or sea-bass, pursue, pierce him with the spear, and hand him to the cook to prepare for dinner. Mr. Nichols was a pious man, and his house was the clerical hotel. The Rev. Mr. Claggett, then Bishop of Maryland, spent a night with us, and I heard him relate the effect which a sermon of the Rev. Geo. Whitefield had on him while a member of the Senior Class in Princeton College. That sermon, he said, determined him to enter the ministry. In company with Mr. Nichols and several of the children, I visited one of his plantations, on the banks of the great Choptank, and there I saw beds of shells several feet deep, and some of them of a most curious formation. I have often regretted that I did not preserve specimens, which might have been of service in the study of conchology.

While at Easton, I visited Baltimore, and had a great fright on the Chesapeake and the Patapsco river. It was a regular squall, such as often occurs in the Chesapeake. We reached the dock without damage.

After remaining with Mr. Nichols a year and a half, I intimated my intention of returning to Princeton. He objected, and proposed giving me four hundred dollars a year for any number of years, with boarding and horse-keeping. I replied, "No! if you gave me four thousand dollars a year I could not stay; I came to you because I was poor, and necessity compelled me to relinquish my studies for a time; I am now in a condition that will enable me to complete my studies. I am pleased with you and your family, and I shall always reflect with pleasure on the relations which we have sustained; but my heart is fixed upon the ministry, and I cannot consent to continue with you any longer." Having procured for him a successor, I prepared to direct my steps to the North. He rode with me nine miles, to two plantations, which he had obtained with his wife, and when we parted, he put into my hand a keepsake, which I found to be a pair of gold sleeve-buttons. He had purchased them when he was married, twenty-two years before, and I have worn them to the present time, (1852.) I received them in May, 1805, so that they have been in use sixty-nine years, and they are at this time in good condition. The family are now nearly all dead, or removed, as I last summer learned from Dr. More, one of my pupils in Easton, who now resides in Philadelphia.

I have many pleasant recollections connected with my residence near Easton, in Talbot county, on the eastern shore of Maryland.

In May I left that hospitable family in company with a number of Friends, who were on their way to attend their yearly meeting in Philadelphia. I was treated as a friend, though I was not a Friend. We parted at Philadelphia, and I proceeded to Princeton, and there tarried a week waiting for the meeting of the Presbytery. I was taken under the care of the Presbytery and entered the class of theological students, under the direction of the Rev. Dr. Kollock, Professor of Theology in the College of New Jersey. Having a few weeks before the Session commenced I made a visit to my mother and family; on my way I called to see her to whom I was engaged, and who afterwards became my wife. The interview was affecting; we had not seen each other for three years and one week. I found my mother and family well; and although suffering from two teeth broken below the gum in attempting to extract them, I was happy in seeing once more the place of my nativity, and the faces of many still familiar to me, though I had not seen them for years.

In a few weeks I returned to Princeton, and commenced my theological studies, in the spring of 1805. The class consisted of Williams, Chapman, Campbell, ———, and myself. We ate at the common table in the refectory. In the fall, at the meeting of the trustees of the college at commencement, I was appointed tutor of the Sophomore class in the college. The other tutor was Mr. Isaac V. Brown. We together had charge of the interior of the college, conducted morning worship in the chapel, and presided at the table in the refectory. One part of our duty was to visit every room twice a day, viz. at two o'clock P. M., and at nine o'clock P. M.

The compensation was a room, fuel, and light, and two hundred dollars a year. And although we were required to remain three hours each day in the recitation room with the Freshman and Sophomore classes, yet we found full as much time for our studies as if we had had no duties to perform in the college. When the bell rang it was a signal for company to depart, or for us to say, "Please excuse us, our class is waiting." The faculty consisted of, Dr. S. S. Smith, President; John Maclean, M.D., Professor of Natural Philosophy and Chemistry; Dr. H. Kollock, Professor of Theology; William Thompson, Professor of Latin and Greek languages; the Rev. Andrew Hauter, Professor of Mathematics and Astronomy; John Johnston, and Isaac V. Brown, Tutors. The faculty were harmonious, with very few exceptions.

In general the students were orderly and attentive to their studies. Occasionally there were proceedings such as are common among lads thus congregated. I recollect that on one night I heard a movement in a certain room, which led me to infer that all was not right. With a light in my hand I went to the room, found the door locked, and was refused admittance. But on announcing my official title, and threatening to break the door unless it was opened, the lights in the room were extinguished, and the door was opened, those within intending to rush out in the dark; but, to their astonishment, I stood before them with a lantern burning. They retreated back, I followed, and having ascertained who they were I advised them to retire to their rooms, and bade them good night. Early in the morning some of them called on me, manifesting considerable uneasiness respecting what they apprehended would be the result. I gave no opinion, but requested all concerned to meet me in one of their rooms immediately after breakfast. I spoke to them respecting the end to which such a course of conduct would lead, and the feelings of their parents and friends if made acquainted with the proceedings of the preceding night. I stated that no one had heard from me one word connected with the subject, and if they would pledge themselves to me that they would abstain from all such conduct in coming time the matter should end. They gave me their word, and I gave each one of them my hand, in token of satisfaction and confidence. The result was far better than if I had reported them to the faculty, and subjected them to the discipline of the college. We often took walks for recreation and health, and on our way we often spent a pleasant hour with Mrs. Dr. Vanclive and her sister, Miss Houston, who afterwards became the wife of my colleague, Mr. Brown.

We were also in the habit of calling to see a pious aged lady, whom we familiarly called "Mother Knox," who said she had heard every one who had been president of the college preach. While she spoke in high terms of all the presidents, the Rev. Samuel Davies was her favorite preacher. Her eyes would brighten on the mention of the name of Davies. Her house was the resort of pious students in the college, and there they would frequently have prayer-meetings, and hear something respecting the interests of religion. There are many still living (1852) that love to remind each other of what they saw and heard in the humble dwelling of Mother Knox.

In connexion with my duties as tutor I acted as assistant librarian. Dr. Kollock and I exchanged the works of the learned Chillingworth for a copy of Guyse's "Paraphrase on the New

Testament," of which there were duplicates in the college library. I also added to my little library King on "The Creed," and Stackhouse's "History of the Bible," purchased from a farmer in the neighborhood.

One evening, while at the head of the table in the refectory, I received a note from Dr. Smith, saying, that two stage loads of Indians had just arrived, and he would introduce them to the students, provided we would keep our seats. In a few minutes they came following the president. They were taken to the library and chapel, and Dr. Maclean showed them drawings of Indians in Cook's "Voyages round the World," and it was amusing to see them run to each other, and then point to the drawings which had some resemblance to one of their company. After a short talk between the president and one of the chiefs, they proceeded through the Campus towards the public house. It was dark, and there were few lights in the windows on the street. Suddenly they raised the warwhoop, and instantly disappeared. Some lay flat on the ground, some concealed themselves behind trees, others at the corners of the houses. After a few minutes they returned to their former station, and commenced a war song as they proceeded to their quarters. It was the most awful and soul-thrilling sound I ever heard. It rang in my ears almost constantly for months, and even now, as I write, I feel a mental agitation. Day after day many of the old and young, black and white, inhabitants of Princeton were endeavoring to act over again the transactions of that evening. The Indians returned to the tavern to sleep, not on a bed but on the floor. The chief of the Little Osage tribe was the most perfect specimen of the human form that I ever saw. He was above six feet high, and in every respect of such proportion as filled the eye with pleasure.

CHAPTER V.

Resigns tutorship—Licensed to preach—Returns to Orange county—Supplies vacant congregations, under the direction of the presbytery of Hudson—Accepts a call from the congregations of New Windsor and Newburgh—History of the church of New Windsor and Newburgh—His marriage—His ordination—Commences housekeeping—Resigns the charge of New Windsor, and gives his whole time to Newburgh—The origin of the church in Newburgh—The ministers who preceded him—The extent of his charge—An infidel club in Newburgh—Ignorance of the religious state of Newburgh—Opposition of friends to his location.

Thus far we have given the autobiography of Mr. Johnston as he has left it, with a few omissions of no importance. He has continued the narrative much further, but it is almost a daily account of his engagements and labors. It is sufficient to know, that he resigned his office of tutor in the college on the last Wednesday in September, 1806, and that he was licensed to preach the gospel by the presbytery of New

Brunswick, in the city of Trenton, on the 8th of October of the same year; that he returned to his native place in Orange county, State of New York; that he received appointments from the presbytery of Hudson to preach in Newburgh, New Windsor, Florida, and Pleasant Valley, all of which congregations were then vacant. In Pleasant Valley there was considerable excitement on the subject of religion, and in a few cases he saw bodily agitations similar to those he had previously witnessed in western Pennsylvania.

He had taken with him only two prepared sermons, intended for the two Sabbaths which by appointment he was to spend in that place. But after the first sermon he found that an appointment was made for him to preach a funeral sermon. And such was the anxiety of the people to hear that he had to preach almost every day, so that he preached thirteen times during the thirteen days that he remained there, besides giving exhortations, or short addresses, at prayer-meetings.

From all the vacant congregations where he

had preached he received invitations to locate himself with them as their pastor. But, for reasons which then appeared to him satisfactory, he refused to permit the congregations of Florida and Pleasant Valley to make out for him formal and regular calls, determined to accept the invitation from the united churches of New Windsor and Newburgh.

When he saw there was a fair prospect of settlement, and of the means of supporting a family, the marriage between himself and Mary Bull, daughter of Daniel Bull, of Orange county, was consummated on the 27th day of January, 1807. They had been born and brought up in the same neighborhood, and an early and mutual attachment had taken place, and they had promised several years before the event occurred to form the relation of husband and wife when, in the providence of God, it might appear to be their duty. Here the strength of Christian principle was manifest, not only in adhering to their sacred vows, but also in that which was more difficult, in not permitting an ardent affection to interfere with the great object in view—preparation for the gospel ministry. During the long interval between their engagement and marriage they were separated from each other, and at one time they had not seen each other for more than three years. This union was long and happy. It was one of those "few happy matches" which, as Dr. Watts expresses it, "were made in heaven." Their natural temperament or disposition was different; not altogether such as Milton alleges between Adam and Eve:

> "Though both
> Not equal, as their sex not equal seemed:
> For contemplation he and valor formed;
> For softness she and sweet attractive grace."

But their natural qualities were such as were exactly suited to each other. The one possessed what the other lacked. He was lively, active, easily moved to mirthfulness or tears, subject to abrupt changes from the highest elevation to the deepest depression. She was calm, sedate, cheerful, not easily thrown from her serene equanimity, not over joyous in prosperity, nor discouraged in adversity; she "kept the noiseless tenor of her way." She was such a wife as Mr. Johnston needed to soothe him in moments of dejection, and to control the exuberance of his feelings in the hours of joy. She was also a helpmate to him in his ministerial work, and contributed largely to his success and usefulness among his people during forty-eight years, as we shall see in the sequel.

Mr. Johnston had preached several times in Newburgh and New Windsor at the close of 1806 and the beginning of 1807. On the 1st of April he began his regular service, although he was not ordained and installed until the 5th of August, 1807. The ordination and installation took place at New Windsor, and the Presbyterial services were performed as follows:

The Rev. Andrew King presided, and made the ordaining prayer; the Rev. Isaac Lewis preached, Col. iii. 11; the Rev. Methuselah Baldwin delivered the charge to the pastor; and the Rev. Ebenezer Grant made an address to the people of the united congregations. They are all gone to their rest.

Mr. Johnston located himself and his companion in Newburgh, occupying a small house in what was then called "the Old Town," in May, 1807, "enjoying," as he records, "in our humble abode as much domestic happiness as falls to the lot of any young clergyman and his companion." In 1813 he had a plain and convenient house erected, on a lot which he had previously purchased, situated in a high and commanding position, from which there is a view of the noble Hudson, the vessels passing and repassing, the elevated range of mountains east of the river, New Windsor, and West Point. He removed into his new dwelling in December, 1813, and resided in the same house until his death. Shortly before his death he remarked, that he knew no family in Newburgh that had occupied the same house so long a time. The congregations of Newburgh and New Windsor were each to have an equal part of his labors, and they engaged each to pay him three hundred and twenty-five dollars a year for his support, making his annual salary six hundred and fifty dollars.

At first he attempted to preach one sermon in each place on the Sabbath, but finding this arrangement on many accounts inconvenient, he afterwards preached a whole Sabbath alternately in Newburgh and New Windsor. As the places of worship were only two miles apart a large part of both congregations attended both services. This arrangement was continued until April, 1810, about three years after his ordination, when, with the consent of both congregations, he was released from the charge of New Windsor, the congregation of Newburgh having presented, through the presbytery, a call for the whole of his services, promising him one hundred dollars more than he had received from both congregations. There he continued to labor until his death.

The life of a settled pastor, especially if he continues to serve the same people for many years, is so uniform and monotonous that it contains few landmarks to variegate and enliven the scenery. Week after week, and year after year, there is the same unvaried routine of parochial duty to be performed, and the same pulpit to be occupied. As with the husbandman, year after year rolls round, each bringing with it the same cares and labors performed in the preceding year. Some seasons are propitious, causing the earth refreshed by rains from heaven, and stimulated by the genial rays of the sun, to produce abundantly. Other seasons, parched with drought or chilled with untimely frosts, are barren and unproductive, when perhaps equal care and labor were expended. If you wish to know whether a farmer has been industrious, and managed his concerns with prudence, or otherwise, you must view his grounds when he first commenced his labors, and at the close of a laborious life notice the improvements he has made, the houses and barns he has built, the rocks and trees he has removed, and the worn out fields he has renovated.

We adopt a similar method in reviewing the ministerial life of Mr. Johnston—

THE FIELD AT THE COMMENCEMENT OF HIS LABORS.

The gospel had been preached in New Windsor at an early period. In his journal the Rev. George Whitefield mentions that he crossed the Hudson and preached at New Windsor. "At the time of my settlement," says Mr. Johnston, "I found two aged females, who considered themselves as the spiritual children of Whitefield. I attended their mortal remains to the grave, the one aged ninety-five and the other ninety-seven. They retained their mental faculties to the close of life, and to their dying day a cheerful smile would play upon their countenance as soon as the name of Whitefield was pronounced." The tradition is, that the Rev. Francis Peppard was the first minister who regularly preached in New Windsor. We have no account that he was installed pastor of that church. During his ministry, a church was organized September 5th, 1766, consisting of eighteen members, by the Rev. Dr. Timothy Johnes, of Morristown, New Jersey. He was called Dr. Johnes, because he practised medicine as well as preached the gospel. This was a common practice with several ministers at that time in East Jersey. The Rev. Jacob Green of Hanover, the Rev. Samuel Kennedy of Baskenridge, and others, sustained the relation of pastor and physician at the same time. From 1773 to 1796, including the trying period of the Revolutionary War, the Rev. John Close preached in New Windsor and in the neighboring places, although he was not installed pastor of the church.

The early records of the church in New Windsor were so imperfectly kept that we do not know what was the success of his ministry; but as it was the harassing time of the Revolution, we are led to believe that the increase of the church was very small. Yet, Mr. Johnston testifies that he found there some aged persons, eminent for their piety, but not one young or middle-aged person either in New Windsor or Newburgh, who was a member of the church. These congregations were for some years under the care of the Presbytery of New York. The congregation of Newburgh was incorporated under the statute of New York in 1784, but no church was organized until 1796, or perhaps 1798, the precise time cannot be ascertained. Before that time, the members of the church living in Newburgh and its vicinity, belonged to the church of New Windsor. The first record which we have of a meeting of the session in Newburgh, was the 26th of April, 1799, at which the Rev. Isaac Lewis presided, and William Lawrence, Abel Belknap, Gilbert Jones, Daniel Birdsall, and Thomas Cooper are named as elders present.

The Rev. Isaac Lewis was stated supply of these congregations about two years, and during that period only one member was added to the church, and that was the wife of Mr. Lewis; and yet Mr. Lewis was a faithful, laborious, and successful preacher in other locations in after life.

The Rev. Jonathan Freeman, the first installed pastor, labored in the congregations of Newburgh and New Windsor from the 5th of May, 1801, to the 25th of April, 1804, nearly three years, and during his ministry thirteen members were added to the church. He was an able theologian of more than common talents, of determined character, sometimes suffering himself to act from the impulse of his feelings rather than from deliberate judgment. He engaged in a newspaper controversy which embittered the feelings of many of the congregation. Imprudent in the management of domestic and secular concerns, he became involved in debt, and this led to his sudden removal. Several pieces which he published show the character of his mind, and the determined course which he was wont to pursue. He was succeeded in the pastoral office in Newburgh and New Windsor by the Rev. Eliezer Burnet, ordained the 20th of November, 1805, and he departed this life on the 22nd day of November the year following, so that his pastoral office continued only one year and two days. He was an amiable, pious, and devoted man, of a feeble constitution. He labored under pulmonary disease at the time of his ordination, and a few months after his settlement he was compelled to travel, and he closed his days on earth at the house of a friend in New Brunswick. Six members, three on examination, and three on certificate, were received as members of the church during his pastorate. As above stated, Mr. Johnston succeeded Mr. Burnet in the charge of the congregations of Newburgh and New Windsor.

These congregations, or rather the people who worshipped in New Windsor and Newburgh, were scattered over a large extent of country, bounded on the north by Balmville and Foster Town, by Gardner Town and the Square on the west, by Cornwall and Canterbury on the south, and by the Hudson on the east, including New Windsor and Newburgh, as well as the villages above named. In all that region, at least eight miles in length and five in breadth, there were only five worshipping assemblies, viz. two Presbyterian, one at New Windsor and one at Newburgh; the Associate Reformed, under the pastoral care of the Rev. Mr. Schrimgeour, worshipping in a building in the south part of Newburgh; and two Methodist, one meeting in the academy, and the other near the turnpike, west of New Windsor. None of these congregations were large, although there were many within the bounds who attended public worship nowhere. In the church in Newburgh there never had been more than sixty-three members.

A few aged persons among these were eminently pious, and mourned over the desolations of Zion. None of the young and unmarried part of the congregations made any pretensions to piety. In Newburgh there were only three places of worship—the Presbyterian, the Associate Reformed, and the Methodist—and no minister residing there. Mr. Schrimgeour, who preached part of his time in Newburgh, resided in New Windsor. In Newburgh there was the frame of a small house, on the same lot where the Presbyterian church now stands, and without galleries or pulpit—the minister having to stand on a carpenter's bench placed on one end of the building. The professors of religion were not only few in number, but the minds of a large portion of the inhabitants were poisoned with infidel sentiments.

At the close of the last century and the beginning of the present there was in Newburgh a regularly organized society of infidels, who met weekly for the purpose of ridiculing the Bible, and of confirming each other in unbelief. They assumed the name of "The Druid Society," and were, in fact, a club associated together in imitation of the societies of the Illuminati, at that time common in Germany and France. They invited to Newburgh a blind man, of the name of Elihu Palmer, and led him to the academy, to deliver to them weekly lectures in opposition to the Bible. This Palmer was an apostate Congregational or Presbyterian minister. He had been educated at Dartmouth college by charity, with a view to the gospel ministry. He preached some time in Pittsfield, Massachusetts, and then removed to Newtown, Long Island; from thence he went to Philadelphia, preached universal salvation, and next gave a weekly lecture on Druidism, and finally he preached deism, or atheism, or anything which, in his opinion, would bring the Bible and its teachings into contempt. This man was brought to Newburgh under a promise of an annual salary, to detail from Sabbath to Sabbath the opinions of Voltaire, Paine, Rousseau, Godwin, and others of the same stamp. A weekly infidel paper was also published in Newburgh. Paine's "Age of Reason," Tyndal's "Christianity as Old as Creation," and other books of the same kind, were reprinted, and circulated with all diligence. These, and similar books, were found in every tavern, or shop, or private house from which they were not positively excluded. These men had also rooms, where obscene prints and pictures were exhibited; and young persons, and even children, were invited and decoyed to view these drawings, which were generally intended to throw ridicule on some portion of sacred history. So bold and outrageous had these infatuated men become, that on a Sabbath after the Lord's Supper had been administered, they collected at a spring near the place of public worship, and, in mockery of what had been done in the church, gave a piece of bread and some water to a dog, using the words of our blessed Redeemer, when he instituted the holy supper. It ought to be known, that the principal actor in this impious transaction did not long survive. On the following Sabbath evening he was found in his room, with the door locked, apparently in a fit. The door was forced, and he was seen lying on the floor, convulsed with awful spasms, and he expired without being able to utter a word. Whether he had taken anything with a view to self-destruction, or whether it was the immediate act of God, without his voluntary agency, we know not. True, a good man may die suddenly, without being able to say a word to surrounding friends; but the proximity of the sudden and awful death of this man to the impious transaction of the preceding Sabbath leads the mind into fearful conjectures. This occurred in July, 1799. In the graveyard in Newburgh there is the following inscription—"The Tomb of —— —— ——, who died July 2d, in the Year of the Christian Era 1799, Aged 34 Years."

On another occasion, a clergyman, after preaching, was attacked by a fierce dog, set on by several persons belonging to the Druid society. For a time it seemed as if these infatuated men had determined that there should not remain in Newburgh and its vicinity a vestige of Christianity; and they employed every means in their power to accomplish their object. But God, in mercy, brought to naught their wicked counsels.*

This society embraced the largest number, and made the most vigorous efforts to propagate its doctrines, between the years 1799 and 1804, but many of its members were still living in 1806, when Mr. Johnston began to preach in Newburgh; and the poison which had been administered in various ways was rankling in the minds of the young, and of many who did not profess to belong to the Druid society. The means which had been used to check the influence of these infidel principles were not judicious, and tended rather to increase than to diminish the evil. There were two weekly papers printed in Newburgh, one called "The Temple of Reason," filled with sarcasms, ridicule, and ribaldry, intended to bring Christianity into contempt; the other a political paper, but willing to publish pieces in defence of Christianity. Two or three writers occupied the columns of this paper for several weeks.

* See Appendix B.

But, however sound and able the arguments, these essays seemed to add fuel to the unhallowed flame issuing from "The Temple of Reason." Ministers who occasionally preached in Newburgh, understanding that infidel sentiments were prevalent in that place, thought they ought to give a prominence to that subject in their discourses, supposing that if they said nothing on the subject it would be an indication of cowardice. Infidel objections to divine revelation were stated in a few words, and a long and, in the opinion of the speakers, satisfactory answer was given. The result was, that the brief objections were remembered, and the labored answers forgotten; and the hearers would retire with the objections fixed in their minds. While these discourses and this process was going on Mr. Johnston was absent in New Jersey, Pennsylvania, and Maryland, making only a few brief visits to his friends in Orange county, twenty miles distant from Newburgh, and of course he was, in a great measure, ignorant of the real state of things in Newburgh when he concluded to fix his residence in that place. His friends, who were better acquainted than he was with the irreligious condition of the place, were greatly distressed when informed that he intended to accept a call from New Windsor and Newburgh. His aged mother wept, and besought him not to locate himself in that wicked place. But although he had not accepted a formal call, he had placed himself in such a position that he thought he could not, without a dereliction of duty, recede. The only word of approbation which he received from any friend was from Daniel Bull, the father of Mrs. Johnston.

In view of the irreligious state of Newburgh, and against the remonstrances of friends, it was a sore trial to adhere to the pledge he had given, and to sacrifice himself in what now appeared a hopeless undertaking. But he dared not to draw back. He has often been heard to say, that if he had known the irreligious condition of the place before he had given encouragement to the people to present a call, his heart would have failed him.

It is thus that the Lord often conceals from

his servants the difficulties and dangers of a work to which he calls them, lest their fears should prevent them from entering the field of labor designed for them. Such was the unpromising field in which Mr. Johnston was called to commence his ministry. It was not from any confidence in his own talents or acquirements that he determined to go forward and meet the gigantic foe. But in an armor as simple and, in human view, as inadequate as that with which David met the Philistine who defied the armies of the living God, he commenced the contest, "not against flesh and blood" only, "but against principalities, against powers, against the rulers of the darkness of this world, against spiritual wickedness in high places."

CHAPTER VI.

His first discourses after ordination—The way he treated infidelity, and the results—Pastoral duties during the first years of his ministry—Catechetical instruction, and Bible classes—Weekly lecture—Revivals in 1812–13, in 1815–16, in 1819–20, in 1824–25, in 1831—New measures—Division of the synod into old and new school—The effect on vital piety—Revival in 1843—The reasons why the number of church members did not increase—Dismissions to other churches given when asked.

THE portions of sacred Scripture with which Mr. Johnston began his ministry in Newburgh indicate his feelings, and the source from which he hoped for success, and also the means which he determined to employ in the work before him.

His first discourse after his ordination was founded on these words: "Brethren, pray for us that the word of the Lord may have free course, and be glorified among you." Implying that he had no confidence in his own strength, that his help must come from God, and that prayer was the means by which that help was to be obtained. The subject of the second discourse was, "I determined to know nothing among you save Jesus Christ and him crucified;" implying that his fixed purpose was to preach the simple and plain truths of the gospel, leaving out of view everything extraneous to salvation, through the merits and mediation of a crucified Redeemer. To this purpose we can say that he strictly adhered, through a long, laborious, and successful ministry of forty-eight years.

It may be asked, "Did he not, in the circumstances in which he was placed, feel it to be his duty to combat and refute, by solid and convincing arguments, the gross infidelity with which he was surrounded?" Not at all. From the beginning he determined not to mention, in the pulpit, the words deist, or atheist, or sceptic, or druid, or free-thinker, or any other name by which the enemies of Jesus Christ and his gospel are designated; but to preach Jesus Christ and him crucified, a balm for every wound, an antidote for every error. He remembered that John Newton had somewhere said, that "the best way to prevent an empty cask from being filled with bad liquor is to fill it with that which is good." And "to overcome error you must keep the attention of the hearer directed to the truth."

Mr. Johnston believed, that "the gospel is its own witness;" that its plain and simple truths find a response in every human heart; that every man who reflects feels that he is a sinner, and that no remedy except that presented in the gospel is adequate to the wants of his soul. He was right. There is a correspondence between the truths revealed in the Bible and the testimony of every man's conscience who gives the subject a serious consideration, more convincing and satisfactory than all logical arguments. This internal evidence, as it is justly called, has in many instances been effectual in convincing and converting infidels, when arguments derived from other sources have utterly failed. Ply a man with arguments addressed to his intellect, and he will find some way to elude their force; but let his conscience speak, and tell him that he is guilty, and he cannot escape from its verdict. He is self-condemned, and he can devise no subterfuge; he is then prepared to listen to the annunciation that "Jesus Christ came into the world to save sinners."

Far be it from us to condemn or undervalue arguments derived from the fulfilment of prophecies, from miracles, from the testimony of martyrs, from the triumphs of the gospel over paganism, over the fury of the populace, and the power of the civil magistrate. Infidels ought to be, and they have often been ably, refuted by arguments, derived from these and similar sources. But in the pulpit, when the speaker addresses a promiscuous audience, arguments requiring much reading and deep reflection to be appreciated, are seldom of any avail. In an ordinary congregation, not more than three or four, or at most half a dozen, of the hearers have the capacity or learning sufficient to follow a long train of argument. But the simple truths of the gospel are intelligible, both to the learned and the unlearned. Both the educated and the uneducated have a heart and a conscience, and they can understand and feel when God, in his word, speaks to them as accountable beings, responsible to him for their thoughts as well as for their words and actions. All fair and honest objections which may arise in the minds of a few reflecting hearers ought to be removed. But this can be more effectually done by private conversation, or by placing in their hands books treating of subjects respecting which they want information. Those few who require their intellect to be satisfied need as much as others the gospel, in its public ministrations, to be brought home to the heart and conscience. And unless it be thus brought home, a mere historical belief that the Bible contains a revelation from God is of little avail.

And what was the result of the course pursued by the pastor in Newburgh? It was soon known that he said nothing in the pulpit respecting deists, or atheists, or Druids, or their doctrines; that he preached the doctrines and precepts which he found in the Bible. "Well," said these free-thinkers, "as we shall not be abused and held up to public odium we will go and hear what he has to say." And the greater part of them did occasionally attend public worship; and all of them, except two, paid the rent of pews for the accommodation of their families, and so contributed to the support of the gospel ministry. And this is not all; the wives, and children, and descendants of several of these bitter enemies of Jesus Christ and his gospel in course of time became hopefully pious, and adorned the doctrine of God their Saviour by holy and exemplary lives. The lives of these men were generally short, and the few who lived to the ordinary age of man were quiet, and said nothing and did nothing to propagate their pernicious principles. There may yet be a few who privately entertain infidel principles, and who read infidel books, but they make no noise, and attract no attention. We may confidently affirm, that now and for several years past there are fewer professed infidels in Newburgh than in any town of equal population in the United States.

We return to the consideration of the pastoral duties of Mr. Johnston. During the first two or three years, after his settlement he did nothing more than attend to the ordinary duties of the pastoral office, and no remarkable effects attended his labors. He preached twice on the Sabbath, visited the sick, attended funerals, and, as had been usual, administered the Lord's Supper twice in the year. After some time he commenced a course of lectures on the Shorter Catechism, and after that, on the Confession of Faith of the Presbyterian Church. These lectures had a salutary effect on himself, and also on his people. They were led to compare the doctrines taught in these symbols with the teachings of the Bible, and excited to inquire on the subject of religion. He also had catechetical and Bible classes, and he encouraged those who attended to ask for explanations of difficult passages, and if prepared, he gave the explanation at the time, and if not prepared, he postponed an answer until the next meeting. These exercises were continued, and were well attended until Sabbath schools were introduced, and then the attendance gradually diminished, and finally the Bible and catechetical classes were broken up, and the reason assigned was, that preparation for the Sabbath school and attendance required so much time that both could not be attended. Although he valued the services of the teachers in the Sabbath schools, he regretted that their instructions prevented him from having a direct influence on the young people of his charge. At first, he had no religious services, except on the Sabbath. After he was released from the congregation at New Windsor, he commenced a prayer meeting in Newburgh on Thursday evenings, which he continued until the close of his ministry. It was at first held in private houses, and in a short time was so numerously attended, that two or three rooms were fully occupied. A lecture room was provided, and it was very soon filled with anxious worshippers; and in the latter part of 1812, nearly six years after his settlement, the first revival ever witnessed in Newburgh commenced. A spirit of prayer was poured out, and an unusual solemnity attended those social weekly meetings. This was the first of seven distinct revivals, which it was the privilege of Mr. Johnston, during his ministry, to witness among the people of his charge. It was the intention of Mr. Johnston to write a full account of those revivals; but it was not accomplished. We shall give the brief notices of these times of refreshing, which we find in various parts of his manuscripts, nearly in his own words. Speaking of the meetings in the session room, he says, "something unusual seemed about to take place. The faith of the people of God was a little strengthened, and some hopes of a revival of religion entertained. As far as I could learn, such a season had never been witnessed in this congregation. Revivals of religion had been heard of, but few among the people had ever witnessed one. Some feared that a revival would take place, others that it would not. A few additions had been made to the members of the church at every communion season, but nothing remarkable had occurred. Our fears and our hopes were alternately excited. At length it was evident in the latter part of 1812 and the beginning of 1813, that the spirit of the Lord was present in his convicting, converting, and comforting influences. The people of God were quickened; a spirit of prayer was felt. It was not then deemed a hardship to go in the shades of the evening to meet for prayer, though there was not then a paved or flagged sidewalk in the whole village. Mud ancle deep was not deemed a sufficient excuse for absence from the prayer meeting. The remembrance of these delightful evenings is still pleasant. They are gone; but the sweet savor they have left excites feelings of joy in the past and desire for a repetition in time to come. Preceding this revival season, one member of the church had turned his attention towards the gospel ministry, and was prosecuting his preparatory studies; and during this revival, another, who is now (1854) actively engaged in proclaiming the unsearchable riches of Christ, resolved to devote himself to the work of the Lord. Another brought into the church at this period, became the wife of a missionary among the aborigines of our own country. And two of the converts of this revival were afterwards set apart to the office of ruling elders in the church. Surely we have just cause of gratitude to God for his loving kindness."

"In the winter of 1815–16, another pleasant season was witnessed. The attention began in the neighborhood of 'the Square,' in the southwest part of the congregation, and gently extended to other parts. For nearly a year, after preaching twice in Newburgh, I had a third service on the Sabbath, and also a lecture on Wednesday evening in the neighborhood of 'the Square.' Persons from several miles around attended, and the largest dwelling house in the neighborhood was not sufficient to accommodate those who assembled. I well remember the visible and real interest taken—the frequent conversations with individuals after the regular exercises—the psalms and hymns and spiritual songs, accompanied with sobs and tears while sung. Then was a time of love, of prayer, and of holy joy. The inquiry, 'what shall I do to be saved,' was succeeded by 'Come all ye that fear the Lord, and I will declare what he hath done for my soul.' While one said, 'Come let us go up to the courts of the Lord,' another said,

'I will go also.' The meetings were often continued until a late hour, and yet I found no inconvenience in returning home alone, five miles, the coldest nights in winter. It was a precious season; the remembrance thereof rejoiceth my soul. We had an addition of between forty and fifty to the church. One of those called from the world, at this time, is a preacher of the gospel, and another a ruling elder."

"Nothing special," continues the record, "occurred during the four succeeding years. About the close of 1819 and the beginning of 1820, the gracious influence of the Holy Spirit was again manifested in the conviction and conversion of sinners. In some respects, that was a season of peculiar interest. There seemed to be a general movement among the dry-bones, and there stood up* as the result of this reviving time sixty-four into whom the Holy Spirit had breathed the breath of spiritual life, accompanied by twenty-two received on certificate from other churches. Two of the hopeful converts became

* See Appendix C

ministers of the gospel, and one a ruling elder in a neighboring church.

"A season of spiritual dearth succeeded this copious shower. In the fall of 1824 I obtained permission to preach in the schoolhouse near the New Mill on the afternoons of the Lord's Day. It soon became evident that the word preached was accompanied with the influence of the Holy Spirit. The interest excited, led several to ask 'what shall we do to be saved?' This special meeting was continued until the 25th of February, 1825, when thirteen were added to the church. Twelve of the thirteen were from the little group of houses near the schoolhouse. Had the awakening been as general throughout the congregation as around the New Mill, more than a hundred would have been pricked to the heart. The sovereignty of God was manifested in confining the work of grace to the small circle around the schoolhouse. But it was a glorious sovereignty, showing how God can accomplish his purposes of mercy towards the church. One of the dozen became a preacher of the gospel, and is now a distinguished minister in the Dutch

Reformed Church. How mysterious and glorious are the dealings of the Lord! *The Lord reigns, let the earth rejoice.*"

"The year 1831 was distinguished among the churches of almost all evangelical denominations for revivals of religion. In conducting them several things took place, and several innovations were made in preaching and in practice, so that this period became proverbial for 'new measures,' some of which might be practised and some might not. Such was the state of public opinion in reference to the proper method of conducting revivals, that it became necessary to comply to a certain extent with prevailing ideas. Compliance on our part, so far as we went, proved a blessing, for which we can never be sufficiently thankful. The subject was laid before the session, and after consultation it was determined to have a four days' meeting, and to invite the attendance and assistance of several ministers, whose labors had been blessed. Special prayer was made and continued several days preceding the meeting. The clergymen who were invited took a deep and lively interest in the welfare of the congregation. We had preaching in the church three times every day, preceded by a prayer meeting of one hour immediately before entering the house of public worship. The morning was ushered in with the voice of prayer. The word was plainly, faithfully, and judiciously preached, and it became quick and powerful—sharper than a two-edged sword, and many of the hearers were pricked to the heart. An awfully solemn stillness prevailed, and the deepest anxiety was felt for the result—it seemed like a week of Sabbaths. Never can I forget the feelings I had when one of the preachers, at the close of one of his sermons, requested all those who had a desire to have conversation respecting their soul's salvation to remain after the blessing was pronounced. The inquiry in my mind was, 'will any remain?' 'who will remain?' The blessing was pronounced—a separation began to take place—some remained—yea many remained. The spirit of the Lord was operating on the minds of the people generally. While many remained in their seats, the majority left the house of God. We have reason to fear that some grieved away the Holy Spirit, and compelled him to depart, never again to return. Methinks I can yet see the agitation, the struggle to overcome the convictions of the Holy Spirit, and an acceptance of Christ and the blessings of his salvation—struggles of some who remained as to the result on their friends who left the place.

"Then was literally repeated what took place in the days of Malachi, thousands of years before—'They that feared the Lord spake often one to another.' Then was the spirit poured forth, and the work of the Lord prospered. Then it was easy to preach, and then there were attentive hearers. Solemnity rested on the minds of the greater part of the hearers, and very few were found to call in question the reality of the work, or to say they were not affected. God was carrying on his work, and man was compelled to say, 'Great and marvellous are thy works, Lord God Almighty.' The fruit of this revival was eighty-three additions to our church on examination, and twenty-two on certificate. And several additions were made to other churches, whence they had come to see and hear, and went away to rejoice, and to engage in the service of the Lord. Of those who united with our church this year two became ministers of the gospel—one a Presbyterian, the other a Methodist. Another commenced studying with a view to the gospel ministry, and his health failing engaged in teaching, and is now at the head of a flourishing female school, in which there is now (1854) a glorious revival of religion. Another young man, received on certificate, after spending a year and a half in the theological seminary at Princeton, apostatized, and was excommunicated. One became a ruling elder; and one a deacon. Of the females who united with our church in 1831 five became the wives of ministers of the gospel.

"The records of the session," Mr. Johnston continues, "show a goodly number of additions to the church at every succeeding communion season, but nothing special occurred for three years. At the communion season in 1834 there was an addition of seventeen; seven of these were received on examination, and ten on certificate. This fact led to the inquiry, 'Why is it that this church owes her increase more to the piety of other churches than to her own?' There must be a cause. This conviction led to self-examination, to greater humility and engagedness in prayer, and to an endeavor to stir up one another to a sense of our situation and duty. In the month of March it was resolved that we would attempt another series of religious exercises, in order to awaken a greater attention to the subject of religion. To provide ministerial assistance I went to New York and Brooklyn, and secured the co-operation of two or three of my brethren. The time for their coming was fixed. Meetings for prayer were appointed, and they continued every evening for a week; and the attendance was greater than usual.

"At the time appointed the congregation assembled; but no clerical brother was present. I felt awfully solemn, in the view of having to attempt preaching myself. If I ever realized my dependence on God it was at that moment. Like minister like people. We all felt solemn, and prayed, and we have reason to believe that

God heard and answered the prayers that were then made, for while we were yet praying the brethren, who had been detained by an unforeseen event, entered the house. Our unbelief was rebuked; our faith was strengthened; our efforts increased. The brethren went to work, and that for several days. We had sermons and prayers morning, noon, and night. If occasionally public service was omitted, it was to afford an opportunity for conversation with those who desired it, while at the same time prayer was made by the church. Conversion followed conversion, and a precious number were able to speak of the wonderful displays of God's mercy and grace to them, and in due time to take up their cross, and publicly to own Jesus Christ as their Lord and Saviour. This was an interesting season, and ought to be remembered with gratitude, and greater diligence and zeal in the service of our blessed Lord and master manifested. Forty-one were received as members of our church—twenty-three on examination; and eighteen on certificate from other churches. Of these one is a minister of the gospel, and two ruling elders.

"But such again was the state of the church, that from February, 1835, to November, 1836, only seven were received on examination, and forty-two on certificate. One of the seven was only thirteen years and fourteen days old, and he is now a minister of the gospel.

"The years of 1837 and 1838 were years of great agitation, not only in Newburgh but in the Presbyterian church throughout the length and breadth of the United States. In 1837 the church was divided, at a meeting of the General Assembly, into what has since been called "the Old School" and "the New School," although the separation did not actually take place with us until the meeting of the synod of New York, in October, 1838. At this meeting it became necessary that each one should decide to which division he would belong. It should be remarked, that in the summer of 1838 a second Presbyterian church had been formed in Newburgh, consisting of twenty-nine members dismissed from the first church, with the cordial approbation of the session and members of the church. When the separation into the Old and

New School took place, the second church went with the New School. This was trying to our feelings, and also to the feelings of several belonging to that church; and at our next communion we had applications from several to be reinstated to their former standing among us.

"When the synod of New York in this place was divided there was great agitation, not only among the members of that body, but also among the people of the congregation. When the vote was taken there was a death-like stillness. Eighty-seven voted to go with the Old School, and forty-one with the New School, and forty-three declined to vote; so that the Old School had three more votes than both the other two sections.

"While these divisions, each claiming to be the synod of New York, were in session, there was a constant passing and repassing of the people from one place of meeting to the other. Curiosity was excited and gratified, but the Holy Spirit was grieved. In some angry passions were roused; in others sorrowful and depressed feelings prevailed, and vital piety languished. The result of the unhappy division in the Presbyterian church was felt for several years. Although we were comparatively free from agitation among ourselves, yet the periodical publications of the day made us acquainted with the unpleasant state of feeling on the subject in other places, and led us to feel, and in some things to speak and to act, perhaps, unadvisedly; and, in the end, led us and others to mourn. But my object is to state facts, and not to make comments, and I dismiss the subject.

"In 1838 one was received as a member who is now a missionary in Northern India. Three were received who became elders in other churches. In 1839 several additions were made to the church on examination and certificate. One, who was afterwards chosen as a ruling elder, but died before the time appointed for his ordination. Two became elders in the church in Newburgh, and one an elder in a church in the city of New York. Two became preachers of the gospel—one a Presbyterian, located in Pennsylvania; one (a colored man) a Methodist.

"In 1840–41–42, several additions were made to our church membership. One, aided by our funds in the theological seminary at Princeton, and licensed by our presbytery, is now a distinguished preacher in one of our cities. Another, received and treated in the same way, has been several years a pastor of a Presbyterian church in western New York. One an elder in this church, and one an elder in the city of New York.

"In consequence of the division," continues Mr. Johnston, "of the Presbyterian church into the Old and New School, the organization of the second church, and its subsequent secession, the passing and repassing of members from the Old to the New School, and from the New to the Old School, the removal of several families from their connexion with our church to another in the village, and the death of one of our most active elders, my mind was greatly depressed, and the state of religion was low. Pastor and people were discouraged; their hands hung down, and their knees were feeble. Truly I can say it was to me a day of darkness and distress. Although I am not conscious of diminishing the number of religious services usually performed, yet these services were attended with an indescribable depression of spirits. Feelings can neither be weighed nor measured, but he who made man well knew that under a smiling countenance and cheerful appearance there lay concealed a bowed down, broken, and distressed heart, which none but God knew or can know. Such was our state in 1842.

"In reviewing the state of the church in 1843 we find an addition to the church of sixty members — forty-eight on examination, and twelve on certificate. We are naturally led to inquire, 'What means were used previous to this large increase?' 'In the time of their affliction,' saith the Lord, 'they will seek me early;' and we found it so. We were made to feel our dependence on God, and we sought his aid by prayer, in the closet, in the social circle, and in public assembly.

"In the month of February we observed the day appointed for prayer in behalf of colleges, and academies, and schools, in order that more of our educated youth might be prepared and disposed to engage in the gospel ministry. The Rev. N. S. Prime, D.D., was with us, and greatly aided in the services of the day, and in the ministerial labors which followed. The season was solemn. The session agreed that a season of special prayer should be observed, and our meetings in the session room continued, with only two or three intermissions, for more than seven weeks. Sometimes we met for prayer, sometimes for conversation, and generally to mingle our sympathies and our joys for what the Lord was doing among us, and to encourage each other to perseverance and Christian duty. When the stated time for the communion drew near, I invited Dr. Prime to be partaker of those festival joys which he had been instrumental in producing. He came, and had his own soul comforted, while he was enabled to comfort others with the comfort wherewith he had been comforted of God. Thus the church was strengthened to trust in the Lord; our weak faith was rebuked; and our benevolent feelings increased and extended to all who love our Lord Jesus Christ, whether they belong to us or to others. Two of those then brought into the church have since been chosen and set apart to the office of ruling elders in this church, and others are occupying important stations in other churches.

"Two or three years after this awakening a particular friend of the church inquired, 'What was the Christian conduct of those who were brought into the church in 1843?' This inquiry led me to sit down, with the list of the names before me, and I was enabled to make such a reply to the inquiry as was highly gratifying to my friend and myself. Perhaps as few, if not fewer, cases were found requiring the interference of the session as among an equal number brought into the church on any former occasion. The church was, at the close of this revival, in a pleasant, peaceful, and united state."

Here we cannot withhold the remark, that Mr. Johnston often spoke of this revival with peculiar interest. It came at a time when it was greatly needed to cheer the desponding heart of the pastor, and of his praying people. He had the co-operation and able assistance of his tried and fast friend, the Rev. Dr. Prime, lately gone to join his brother, where prayer, and faith, and preaching are not needed, to rejoice together in the retrospect of their mutual labors, and to enjoy the approving smiles of their blessed Redeemer.

"The youngest member admitted to the church was nine years and three months and twenty-three days. The oldest eighty years. And the exercises of their minds were various. In general there was a deep conviction of sin, commencing, perhaps, with a view of some particular sin, and extending to others, and finally leading to a view of the depravity of the heart and a consciousness of entire helplessness and dependence on the sovereign mercy of God. Sometimes there was terror, and apprehension of divine wrath; sometimes there was no fear, but merely a sense of sinfulness in the sight of God, and of hardness of heart and distress because they were not alarmed. The work of conviction continued a longer or a shorter time, and some, under remorse of conscience, never obtained peace by accepting of a free salvation, through faith in the Lord Jesus Christ. One young woman was greatly distressed because she had no conviction of sin.

"In the year 1844 nineteen were added to the church—one half on examination, and the other half on certificates from other churches. Since 1843 there has been no special movement or ingathering into the church worthy to be denominated a revival. But there have been additions on examination at almost every communion season, though the greater part have been on certificates from other churches. There has also been a uniform and respectable attendance on public worship in the house of the Lord. We have enjoyed peace and quietness among ourselves, and with Christians of other denominations. We may add that we have done something, though less than we ought to have done, for the glory of God, by contributing of our worldly means to send the gospel to the destitute in our own and in foreign lands, as well as aiding various other benevolent objects."

Such is a brief account of the revivals with which the Lord blessed the labors of his servant in Newburgh, selected from various parts of his manuscripts.* At the time of the separation of the church of Newburgh from that of New Windsor there were only thirty-seven communicants in the church of Newburgh. The number added to that church during his ministry we have not been able satisfactorily to ascertain. It must have been large. From statistical reports to the general assembly it appears there were sometimes as many as four hundred communicants. In late years there have been only between two hundred and fifty and three hundred. This diminution in numbers did not arise (as is evident from the additions yearly made) from a decline in piety, but from the migratory character of the inhabitants. There was a time when the trade of the fertile counties of Orange, Ulster, Delaware, and Sullivan centred in Newburgh, or passed

* Some things peculiar, respecting members of the church, will be found in Appendix F.

through it to New York. Since the opening of railroads and canals, a great change has taken place in the course of business. Some, who did not succeed according to their expectations, removed to new settlements; others, who had increased their capital, passed down to the city of New York, the great emporium of trade; some, for want of accommodations in the Presbyterian church, went to other churches in Newburgh, and others were dismissed to form a second Presbyterian church. These movements diminished the number of communicants and impaired the strength and efficiency of the Presbyterian church in Newburgh. But these changes were probably the means of promoting the general interests of the Redeemer's kingdom. The dismissed members carried with them the previous zeal which they had imbibed in Newburgh, and formed the nuclei around which other churches were collected. Such facts were more than once brought to the knowledge of their former pastor, and rejoiced his heart—and in the spirit of the forerunner of our Lord, he could say: "He must increase, but I must decrease." It seems to be the order of the divine government, that Christians should not be collected together in one place, but be scattered abroad over the face of the earth as the husbandman sows his seed. The first converts to Christianity were not permitted to remain long in Jerusalem, but driven by persecution to various places, they conveyed with them the good tidings of salvation.

It may as well be remarked in this connexion, as elsewhere, that the Session of the Presbyterian church in Newburgh, gave without hesitation, a dismission to any member in good standing who requested it, to unite with any other church in the place. This liberal policy was reciprocated by all the churches in Newburgh, except the Episcopal. On the first application for a dismission from that church, to join the Presbyterian, the applicant was informed that a certificate of dismission was in such cases never given, and if any member chose to leave the Episcopal church on his own responsibility his name would be removed from the roll of communicants without farther censure. After this announcement, no certificate was asked from persons coming from that church.

CHAPTER VII.

The means used to watch over the members of his church, and to keep himself acquainted with the state of his congregation —Emmonism—Change of views and practice in baptizing children and adults—Re-baptizing Roman Catholics—Efforts to educate young men for the gospel ministry—The Wills of Robert and Marion Hall, and Gilbert King, establishing the Ed and King Scholarship in the Theological Seminary of Princeton—Ministers' wives—Church music.

MR. Johnson did not labor to increase the members of his church, and then leave them to be governed and edified by the general instructions given in public ministrations of the word and ordinances. Like a good shepherd, he watched over his flock, and applied to individuals such attention as their wants required. His predecessors had been in the habit of administering the Lord's Supper only twice a year; this custom he saw cause to change, and he administered this ordinance four times in the year, once on a fixed day in every quarter, so that those in the remote parts of the congregation who from age or infirmity, or any other cause, could not attend public worship every Sabbath, might know the season of communion and make arrangements to be present.

Before each communion, the Session met, and the roll of the members was read over, and if any of the elders knew any member whose conduct or state of mind required particular attention, it was made known to the pastor, and in this way he was kept acquainted with the wants and circumstances of every member of his church, and was prepared to administer such consolations or reproofs as each case demanded. This was done by private conversation, in which he was peculiarly happy, or by placing in the hands of individuals such tracts or books as were suited to the case. He made frequent use of the publications of the Assembly's Board, and he often spoke of these books as an inestimable blessing to his people: and they manifested their estimation of the value of the work by liberal annual contributions to sustain it.

The same occasions were also improved to ascertain the state of mind or conduct of those belonging to the congregation who were not members of the church, so that in his parochial visits and preaching the pastor might accommodate his conversation and preaching to the condition of the people. This practice, when conducted with prudence, cannot be too highly recommended. It excites the elders to vigilance and care, and enables the pastor to adapt his instructions to the wants of his charge.

At one period, the mind of Mr. Johnston was greatly annoyed and perplexed by the peculiar doctrines of Dr. Emmons. In his congregation there was one man of considerable intelligence, who had fully embraced the views of Emmons, and he was zealous in propagating them by conversation and by circulating books on the subject. He urged with great importunity on the pastor himself these sentiments. Mr. J. was compelled to give the subject a full examination, with a determination to follow the truths of the Bible to whatever conclusions they might lead him; at the same time, as he had given his assent to the doctrines contained in the confession of faith of the Presbyterian church, he resolved that he would preach nothing contrary to that standard as long as he remained a minister in that church, and if he found the doctrines in which he had been educated, erroneous, he would withdraw from the Presbyterian church. Such was the ingenuity of the reasoning of Dr. Emmons, that, admitting his premises, it was difficult to resist the conclusion. After stating his perplexities, Mr. J. adds, "I have reason to be thankful that Dr. Emmons was the man who relieved me from my perplexities and led me to a settled peace, which has never been disturbed from that time. In the 14th sermon of one of his volumes on this text—'Be it known unto you men and brethren, that through this man is preached the forgiveness of sins,' he proposes to show—1st. What is forgiveness; 2d. What is forgiveness for Christ's sake; and 3d. That forgiveness is the only blessing we receive for Christ's sake. This last head he labors at great length, and then proceeds to infer that forgiveness is the only blessing we receive for Christ's sake; that sinners are not justified for Christ's sake; also, that it is wrong for ministers to direct sinners to Christ for faith, repentance, &c. As I read, the thought flashed on my mind—is not Christ exalted to give repentance as well as the remission of sins? Did not one say?—'Lord, I believe; help thou my unbelief.' Are we not justified freely by his grace, through the redemption that is in Christ Jesus? I will believe God, and I was at rest, and was never afterwards disturbed by the subtleties of Dr. Emmons or any of his followers."

On the subject of baptism, the practice of Mr. J. underwent a change. We give a statement on this subject in his own words. "When," says he, "I was introduced into the ministry, I had no settled principle respecting the proper subjects of baptism. In the congregation where I was located, it was usual to admit persons of adult years to baptism, who refused or neglected to come to the Table of the Lord. It was also the custom for parents to have their children baptized when neither of them were in full communion with the church. My pastor in the days of my childhood, the minister who admitted me to the communion of the church, and the professors under whom I studied theology, all practised on what in New England is called the 'half-way covenant.' I commenced and continued my ministry in the same way, until I was invited to baptize in a private way the child of parents who I was well persuaded were not only immoral, but grossly immoral, though it was not known to the public. My conscience condemned me, and I resolved I would not do the like again. To fortify myself before my people, I preached several sermons on the nature of the engagements, into which persons who offered their children in baptism entered, and the force of these obligations. In conclusion, I informed my people of the change my own sentiments had undergone—that hereafter I would baptize no adult who was not prepared to become a member of the church in full communion; and that I would baptize no child unless one or both of the parents were members of the church in full communion. I moreover stated that I wished every one carefully to examine the subject, and if any one after examination was still of the opinion that the former practice was right, I was willing to exchange with any brother minister who thought it right to practise as we had heretofore done. I do not recollect that I ever had a serious application from any of my people to depart from my determination. In one or two cases another minister came, and without my knowledge administered baptism to a few children. The parents honored my candor and took no offence." Whether this change in sentiment and practice was right or wrong, it manifested great tenderness of conscience, and also Christian prudence in making the change in such a way as not to alienate the minds and affections of his people.

In another particular touching baptism Mr. Johnston differed from the usage of many in the Presbyterian church, and from the decision of the General Assembly in the following way:—

A missionary under the care of the Presbytery of Hudson, located in Buenos Ayres, wrote to his Presbytery to direct him what to do in the case of persons entering the Protestant from the Roman Catholic church. The Presbytery was divided in opinion, and referred the subject to the Synod of New York. The Synod, after discussing the subject two days, referred it to the General Assembly, and the General Assembly decided that such persons ought not to be re-baptized—chiefly on the ground that, although that church was grossly corrupt in doctrine and practice, it still maintained some fundamental doctrines of the gospel, and had in its communion many pious persons, and ought to be regarded as a church of Christ. Mr. Johnston viewed that church in a different light; and great as his respect was for the decisions of the General Assembly, he re-baptized in several cases persons coming from the Roman church and entering the Presbyterian.

The great object which occupied the mind and interested the heart of this good man, next to the spiritual welfare of his people, was the preparation of young men for the gospel ministry. He believed that if he could be the means of bringing forward young men of piety and talents, and of preparing them for the work of the Lord, he would do more good than he could do in any other way; and we are happy to say that in this respect his efforts were eminently successful. Whenever he found a young man in his church of piety and promising talents, he talked to him on the subject, and if he was doubtful respecting the talents of any one who was desirous of devoting himself to the work of the ministry, he made trial of his gifts and capacity to receive mental culture by giving him instruction for a short time, and when he came to a favorable conclusion he encouraged his pupil to commence a regular course of study. Some of the young men who studied, were able, through the means of their parents and friends, to pay the expenses of their own education; others were poor, and had no means of support except the labor of their hands. In the latter case their pastor assured them that means would be provided if they showed themselves worthy of support. He did what he could himself, and his good people were not slow to follow his example. The females of his charge were induced to form cent societies, and sewing societies, and reading societies, and from these little circles clothing was provided, and money collected to pay for tuition, and perhaps boarding was furnished by parents while their sons were preparing to enter college.

By the aid of the Assembly's Board of Education, and other societies, Mr. Johnston devised ways and means to support several through a full course of collegial and theological studies. In one case it is known to us that Mr. J., with a family of ten children of his own, took the son of a poor man who had removed to the West, boarded, and clothed, and paid tuition bills, until the youth was fitted for college, receiving from the Board of Education only sixty-five dollars a year. Among his manuscripts we find the names and a brief history of twenty-two members of his church, who became ministers of the gospel, and some of them missionaries in heathen and foreign lands. Others are occupying places of usefulness in our own country. Of all who were encouraged to prepare for the gospel ministry, only one turned out badly. This young man had been received on certificate from another church, and was only a short time a member of the

Presbyterian church of Newburgh. That so few disappointed the hopes of their patron, is a proof of a sound judgment in making the selection. Before the time of Mr. J., not one young man in the congregations of Newburgh and New Windsor had turned his attention to the ministry; indeed, there was no unmarried person, male or female, belonging to either of these churches when he took charge of them. So fully was our departed brother convinced of the importance of a thorough education, that he encouraged no one to seek the ministry who had not determined to take a full course of literary and theological studies. When a proposition was sent down from the General Assembly to the Presbyteries to ascertain whether or not it was their wish to establish a theological seminary, every member of his Presbytery, except himself, voted against the proposal. He saw the importance of such an institution, and he advocated it, and from that day until his death he was its firm and zealous supporter. Through his instrumentality two scholarships, of twenty-five hundred dollars each, were founded in the seminary at Princeton, and the nomination of those who should have the benefit of these scholarships was vested in the Session of the First Presbyterian church in Newburgh. So that when a young man, a member of that church, was prepared to enter the Seminary, provision was ready for his support. In this way, several useful and some distinguished ministers of the gospel have been carried through a full course of theological study; and as the interest only of the scholarships is expended, the same process may be continued until it shall not be necessary for "one to say unto another know the Lord, for all shall know him from the greatest to the least."

One of these scholarships was founded by Robert Hall and his sister Marion. They were natives of Scotland, had been brought up under the ministry of the Rev. John Brown of Haddington, and had been employed a great part of their lives in teaching in Scotland and in this country. When Mr. Johnston, of whose church they were members, understood they wished to dispose of their property for the education of pious young men for the gospel ministry, he suggested establishing a scholarship in the theological seminary at Princeton; and it was done, and the money was paid by the executors to the treasurer of the General Assembly. As there is something peculiar in their Will, we give the following extract. "We give and bequeathe twenty-five hundred dollars to the Rev. John Johnston, the Rev. Joseph McCarroll, Mr. John Forsyth, and Mr. John Beveridge, all of the town of Newburgh, county of Orange, and state of New York, the survivor or survivors of them, their heirs, executors, administrators, or assigns, for ever for the use of and in trust for the trustees of the General Assembly of the Presbyterian church in the United States to be applied to the benefit of the theological seminary of the said church, and now located at Princeton, in the state of New Jersey. Further it is our will that this sum of twenty-five hundred dollars be funded by the trustees of the General Assembly, and that the interest alone be annually expended. And whereas after a life of nearly four score years (much of which has been spent in examining the word of God) we are fully satisfied of the correctness of the doctrines of religion as laid down in the confession of faith, the larger and shorter catechisms drawn up by the Westminster Assembly of Divines, and as held by the General Assembly of the Presbyterian Church in the United States, we desire that the scholarship which is endowed by this bequest of $2500, shall be called the Ed* Scholarship, as a witness between us and the theological seminary, that the Lord he is God agreeably to said confession of faith and catechisms. Further it is our will that the professors in said seminary be careful that no person holding sentiments inconsistent with the confession of faith, larger and shorter catechisms, be ever admitted to the benefit of said scholarship. And further it is our will that the session of the first Presbyterian church in Newburgh, county of Orange, and state of New York, possess the right of naming the student who shall enjoy the benefit of said scholarship, provided he be received into the seminary agreeably to the restrictions of the former para-

* Joshua xxii. 34.

graph." It was a subject of pleasure to these pious people to think on their deathbed that their property would be aiding in educating ministers after they were dead and gone. They are interred side by side in the common burying ground in Newburgh. The old lady said, if anything was put upon her head-stone, it should be, "To know as I am known; I know not: but I am ganging to know."

Mr. Gilbert King, a member of the church in Newburgh, at the suggestion of his pastor, also endowed a scholarship in the seminary at Princeton, giving the Session of the Presbyterian church in Newburgh the right of naming the beneficiaries. This scholarship became productive in 1837. Mr. King came from Long Island to Orange county, New York, and for many years followed the business of shoemaking. Having sold a small farm on which he lived in the country, he came to Newburgh that he might enjoy the privileges of the gospel. He became a member of the Presbyterian church, and spent the evening of his days in communion with God and his people.

His remains are interred in the old church grave-yard in Newburgh.

From the commencement of the Theological Seminary at Princeton, until his death, Mr. Johnston's whole heart was engaged for its interests, and through his influence his people contributed liberally every year for the support of the professors, before professorships were endowed, as well as for other wants of the institution. In 1817, he was chosen a director, and he continued a director until his death, being re-elected every third year. He punctually attended the meetings of that Board, and was often one of the examining committee at the close of the sessions.

Believing that the Christian training of young females was not less important than that of young men, Mr. Johnston took special care to give their minds such a direction as would prepare them for usefulness in the church of God. And it is a remarkable fact and worthy of notice, that eighteen members of his church were married to ministers of the gospel, and three of that number went as missionaries to heathen lands.

In the memoranda before us, we have the names and a brief history of the eighteen females who were intimately connected with the interests of the church. Where, we may ask, has any church under the ministry of one man furnished so many laborers in the Lord's vineyard?

Mr. Johnston had a taste for music, and he considered singing one of the most delightful and profitable parts of public worship. His own children had fine voices, and he took care that they should be cultivated in the best manner. In his daily family worship the singing was charming, and his daughters aided greatly in the music of the public sanctuary. We give his own account of this part of worship, when he came to Newburgh, and of its improvement:—"When," says he, "I took charge of the congregation, an old gentleman, one of the elders, was leader; he had neither voice nor taste, was ignorant of all the rules of music, and his performance was sufficient evidence of all this. A music teacher was afterwards employed, and he led the music during his continuance. When he left we were as ill off as ever, nay worse; for some began to see and feel the necessity of cultivating church music, and began to complain of its performance in public worship. A bass-viol was presented by a member of the church, on condition it would be used in public worship. A choir was formed, and the viol was used, and the congregation was well pleased. Unfortunately, however, a good old Scotch woman, who had been delighted with the music for several Sabbaths, one day going out of the church, happened to see the bass-viol, and was horrified. She came to see me on Monday morning, complimented me for my sermon, but, said she, all the good impressions it made were driven out of my head by the vile thing I saw in the gallery—and then with much feeling she exclaimed:—'Oh! Mister Johnston, did I think I would ever live to see a fiddle in the house of God?' She took her departure, and she never again united with us in public worship. The bass-viol was continued for several years in connexion with the choir. At length the viol was dropped, and the choir leads the music to the present time (1852), and I have no hesitation in saying we have the best performance in church music of any congregation in the circle of my acquaintance. And this also has been the testimony of clergymen and others who have worshipped with us."

CHAPTER VIII.

Efforts to organize a Second Presbyterian church in Newburgh —Extract of an address on that subject—The result—The Second church becomes New School, and is dissolved —The increase of churches in Newburgh—Improvement in morals—Drs. Brown and McCarroll—The extent of the original Presbytery of Hudson—Vacant congregations and supplies—Hudson Presbytery divided, and North River Presbytery formed—Bedford Presbytery formed from North River Presbytery—Two New School Presbyteries formed from these—Increase of ministers—Punctuality in attending Presbytery and other judicatories of the church—Fourteen times a Commissioner to the General Assembly—A delegate to the General Association of Connecticut and of Massachussets—A delegate to the General Association of New Hampshire and General Convention of Vermont—Biography of 140 ministers—Records of the Presbytery of Dutchess —Elected a Trustee of the College of New Jersey—The degree of Doctor in Divinity conferred.

An extract from a discourse delivered to his people early in 1838, will show the state of things and the wishes of the pastor:—"Permit me to call your attention to a particular subject, and which has long pressed heavily on my mind —I mean the organization of a Second Presbyterian church. On this subject I have often spoken in public and in private, and I have as often met with objections and a backwardness to engage in the work. The consequence has been, that while other congregations have arisen and increased, ours has remained stationary. I do therefore beg leave once more to state my views, and to solicit your candid attention.

"In the first place I premise that I am not conscious of being actuated in this matter by any ill will towards any Christian denomination in this place; I can honestly say that I wish them all well, and it gives me pleasure to learn that God is glorified in these different churches, in the purity, prosperity, and increase of their members. But I am a Presbyterian, and as such, I have a partiality towards the Presbyterian church, and in saying so, I express towards her the feeling of others towards the church of their choice. Their preference is seen in the course pursued, and so should mine and yours be also. Let us now look at a few facts. When I came to this place thirty-one years ago, our house of public worship had no gallery, and was not so large as it now is, and of course it could not accommodate as many as it now does. I very well remember, that in the summer after I came, benches had to be introduced into the aisles to accommodate the hearers. The number of hearers increased so, that the second year a gallery was erected, and the house was finished, and the congregation then called for the whole of my time. The year following I was released from the congregation of New Windsor, and the house was again filled; and I appeal to some of the aged if they do not remember the numerous congregation that was in attendance from Sabbath to Sabbath. The Episcopal church then went up, and this took away our surplus members; and it was only a year or two before we found our want of seats. Then the Associate Reformed church was erected in the place where it now stands, and several of our congregation went there, as accommodation could not be had with us. The Covenanter church went up, and took from us several of our number. Our church admitted of being enlarged and altered, so as to accommodate a larger audience than heretofore. This enlargement was made; and when the seats were disposed of, there were fourteen families that were not accommodated. Some of these found places by sharing a pew with others, and some left the congregation. This occurred ten years ago; the consequence has been that no increase in the congregation could take place, for if a family came in another must go out. Thus, for want of room, many who gave a preference to the Presbyterian church, were compelled to go to places of worship where they had not intended to go. This is a difficulty which has prevented people from making Newburgh their residence. I could name a very respectable man, who, in conversation with me, assigned this very thing as the reason of not locating his family in this village. I do verily believe that several churches in this place have received additions, and have, to a considerable extent, been built up of materials that wished to remain Presbyterian. I have known families to remain for years without forming a connexion with other churches, and afterwards were disappointed in their wishes. Applications are still made from time to time, without success. Only think of this congregation, the same now as to numbers that it was twenty-nine years ago, while the population of the place has increased more than three-fold. Churches of other denominations are springing up and multiplying, and the Presbyterian remains the same. Now, other denominations are not to be blamed; they are to be commended—the fault is ours; we are the sufferers. We have not the same stimulating causes to urge us forward; exertions are not made to bring in those who do not attend any place of worship; and if they were made where can you offer them a seat? Individuals may feel anxious to enlarge our borders, but in order to success there must be concert and union. Again, look at the effect on the young and rising generation. They are not called to activity and exertion in the cause of Christ, and they grow up in ignorance of their privileges and duties; and if stirred to do something they must seek some other place. While an opportunity is given them to exert themselves in other enterprises, none is furnished for exertion to build up the church of God, unless they go out from their father's house.

"There is another evil arising out of our supineness. We are insensibly changing the ecclesiastical relation of our families. Here is a parent with a rising family sufficiently numerous to fill his seat; a son is married, and no place is found for his accommodation. He has been accustomed to attend public worship—(for, my hearers, this is a church-going people) but where shall he go? He must leave the house in which he was brought up, and the mode of worship that he prefers, and unite with another people. In due time another member of the family is in the same situation, and after awhile the entire family is gone. I could name families where this process is going on, and where the result before long will probably be as we have stated. The wealth of this congregation is greater than that of any other in the place, and enough could be spared without any inconvenience to establish another congregation on a foundation that would promise permanence and usefulness. Moreover, there is talent and capacity for usefulness beyond what is demanded in one congregation, and which needs only to be brought into operation to be useful. Furnish the opportunity, and the result will rejoice your hearts. But it is one thing to urge the accomplishment of an object, and another to point out how it can be done. Before I proceed, permit me to say, after a pastoral relation of thirty-one years, I can here bear testimony to your kindness, and the expressions of that kindness both to myself and to my family; and while I desire ever to feel a deep sense of your kindness, I am not conscious of a wish to be disconnected from any family in the congregation. If it be the will of God that my usefulness may continue as long as I remain on the earth, I desire to live and die with you; but if the prosperity of the Redeemer's kingdom require it, I am ready to part with any number of families that may choose to withdraw and unite in building up a second Presbyterian church. With these remarks I submit my plan. Let there be encouragement given to the younger part of the congregation to engage in this noble enterprise. Here are young men commencing the business of life,—they are young, active, and enterprising; let them have an opportunity of exerting themselves in laying up durable treasures in helping forward the kingdom of Christ. Here are rich individuals who have sons, or nephews, or friends; say to them:—'subscribe a thousand or five hundred dollars, or any other handsome sum, and I will pay it. What I want is, that you take an active part in building up a second Presbyterian church and congregation.' Oh! how do you know, but that God will make this the means of enlisting the energies of your sons in the noblest work, and of leading them to the Saviour? Thus you may prepare the way for them to do good, while you remain where you are. But it may be said, those churches will become rivals. Rivals! What a glorious rivalship—sons endeavoring to outdo their fathers in building up the kingdom of the blessed Redeemer! Relatives vieing with each other for the honor of bringing the greatest number of souls to a saving and eternal relationship to the Lord Jesus Christ. Here it seems to me are a great many young men who are waiting for an opportunity of engaging in the work of the Lord. Now it will not do to say to children and young persons, go!—but we must say, here is a portion of the goods which I intend for you, and it is my wish, that the first fruits of my bestowment should be consecrated to the Lord. Oh! my friends, it will afford you satisfaction in a dying hour, to reflect that a part of the property which the Lord has given you, has been thus consecrated to his service. Should such an enterprise be now attempted, I hope to see a young man settled as a co-presbyter, and I shall look for aid from him in building up the church of God. Let me say, I greatly desire to see another Presbyterian church in this place before I go hence. This subject was under consideration last year, and approved by the officers and such of the congregation as were present at the meeting for consultation, yet nothing was done. Let us try once more."

This was a noble and effective address, worthy the occasion, and characteristic of the man who delivered it. He utters no expression of envy or jealousy on account of the increase and success of other churches, but rather of congratulation. He indicates no narrow, selfish desire to retain as large a number of hearers and supporters as possible. He is willing and desirous to resign the young and hopeful part of his charge, provided the kingdom of Jesus Christ be extended and built up according to the doctrine and discipline which he believes is most in harmony with the word of God. The result of this effort was, that a second Presbyterian congregation was organized, and twenty-nine members of the old church were dismissed to form the beginning of the new. As has been already stated, a majority of this church and congregation after the division of the Synod into the Old and New schools at Newburgh, voted to connect themselves with the latter. Some, dissatisfied with this arrangement, returned to their former place, and some went to other churches. The first pastor of the second church was the Rev. William Hill, installed October the 19th, 1841, and he was deposed in

1844, by his Presbytery, for strenuously maintaining that perfection in holiness was attainable, and was actually attained by believers in this life. The Rev. John Gray succeeded as a stated supply, and after three or four years, left. The congregation was involved in a heavy debt, and their house of worship was sold, and is now occupied by the Second Methodist Society. Since the time of Mr. Johnston's settlement, the number of places of public worship in Newburgh has increased four-fold, and there has been a corresponding improvement in morals and piety. There are very few families in the place that are not nominally connected with some religious society. The Sabbath is decently observed. The streets are quiet, and the people generally attend some place of public worship. The taverns are better regulated than in many places; respectable hotel keepers refuse to sell intoxicating drinks to inhabitants of the place on any day in the week, consequently there is no lounging in the bar-rooms and carousing at night, disturbing the rest of travellers and boarders. Open infidelity has disappeared. Universalists, Unitarians,

Mormons, and similar sects, have no foothold in Newburgh; and if it were not for the Roman Catholics, who came to the place to labor on railroads, and at the wharves, very little profane swearing would be heard in the streets. The people of Newburgh are a church-going and a moral people; such was formerly not the fact. Infidel publications were scattered there broadcast; intemperance, and drinking to intoxication, even at funerals, was not uncommon; the Lord's Day not regarded, and children without instruction or restraint permitted to run in the streets on that sacred day. We are far from claiming for any one man, the honor of this reformation and increase of piety. To Mr. Johnston belongs the honor of commencing the work, and of continuing longer in the field than any other. Able and faithful coadjutors of other denominations, in the progress of time, came to his aid, and labored with him harmoniously and successfully in pulling down the strongholds of Satan, and in building up the kingdom of Christ.* More than fifty Protestant ministers preached a

* See Appendix D.

longer or a shorter time in Newburgh during the ministry of Mr. Johnston, and he never had a quarrel or angry word with one of them. Towards the close of life, he often spoke of the uninterrupted harmony and friendship that existed between himself and the Rev. Dr. John Brown, of the Episcopal church, and the Rev. Dr. Joseph McCarroll, of the Associate Reformed church.* With the former he lived and preached in the same village thirty-nine years, and with the latter thirty-three years.

We have seen the progress of piety and good morals in the first Presbyterian church, and also in the village of Newburgh; let us look at the Presbytery of Hudson, and the region over which it extended. This Presbytery, at the time Mr. Johnston became a member, extended from the bounds of the Presbytery of Albany on the north to Manhattan island on the south, and from the border of Connecticut on the east to the Delaware river on the west. In this extensive region, in 1807, there were only six settled Presbyterian ministers, and two superannuated without charge; and there were a large number of small

* See Appendix E.

congregations vacant. The Presbytery had no licensed preachers under its care; these congregations must be left without hearing the gospel, or ministers who had charges of their own must occasionally leave their people and preach in these destitute places. At the semi-annual meeting of Presbytery, as many as two or three appointments were made for each minister, and he was required to report at the next meeting whether or not he had fulfilled them. Mr. Johnston seldom failed—not long before his death he recorded that in forty-eight years he had not three times disappointed the people to whom he had promised to preach. Frequently he had to go on horseback through rain and snow, a considerable distance, to fulfil these appointments. Sometimes he was absent four or five days in fulfilling an appointment.

In 1812, he was sent by his Presbytery as a missionary to spend *three* or *four* weeks, near what was called the Cook-house, now Port Deposit. After travelling sixty miles he came to the Delaware, at Coshocton, crossed the river, and rode up the river forty or fifty miles, and preached in several places. The country through which he passed was wild and dreary. In one place he went twelve miles through the woods without seeing a house or the mark of an axe. He felt gloomy; but when he came to the place where Brainard had preached to the Indians, his heart revived, when he compared the privations and labors of that devoted man with his own. On his way up, he lodged with a widow lady, with whom he had an interesting conversation.* During his journey, it rained incessantly for two days, yet he proceeded and fulfilled his appointments. On his return he put his horse on a raft of timber prepared for the Philadelphia market, and came with great rapidity forty miles down the river near to the place where he had crossed going up. This journey, he remarked, gave him some idea of the hardships and sufferings of those who commence settlements in new countries of a missionary life.

Returning from this excursion and from preaching in other destitute places, he usually

* See Appendix G.

felt dejected, believing his labor was all lost. He seemed like a man who scattered good seed in an uncultivated forest, and who left it to rot, or to be picked up by birds, or to be choked by surrounding vegetation. But his unbelief was rebuked by learning before he left the world that happy results had followed in a few cases where no success was anticipated. And it is not improbable that many more of the same kind will be ascertained where he is now gone.*

In 1819, the Presbytery of Hudson had so increased that a division was thought necessary. The Hudson river was to form the general boundary. But in order to make the parts more equal, three ministers (of which Mr. Johnston was one) and three congregations on the west side of the river were connected with the eastern division called "The North River Presbytery." A few years after the Presbytery of Bedford was formed from the southern part of the Presbytery of the North River. When the division into the Old School and New School in 1838 took place, two New School Presbyteries were formed with-

* See Appendix H.

in the bounds of the original Hudson Presbytery. And instead of six or eight ministers, as was the case in 1807, there were in 1854 eighty-nine settled ministers or stated supplies. And within the bounds of the "North River Presbytery" there were no vacate congregations. How great the change during the ministerial life of one man! In attending the meetings of Presbytery and other judicatures of the church, Mr. Johnston was a model of punctuality. At an early period he was appointed stated clerk of the Presbytery, and he seldom failed to be present at the hour appointed, bringing the records of the Presbytery with him. He was fourteen times a commissioner to the General Assembly of the Presbyterian church, and he never failed to attend, and we find among his manuscripts a record of the transactions of that body.

In 1814, he was chosen by the General Assembly a delegate to attend the General Association of Massachusetts; and again, in 1826, he was appointed by the same body a delegate to the General Association of New Hampshire, and the General Convention of Vermont. In both cases he travelled on horseback, called on many distinguished clergymen, and visited the principal towns and cities in New England. He left a journal of these tours, in which many interesting facts are recorded.

The large heart of this good man was not confined to the limits of his own congregation or Presbytery, or even General Assembly of the Presbyterian church. His benevolence embraced the whole family of man. He was the ardent friend of foreign and domestic missions; within his appropriate sphere he successfully labored to promote them, whether conducted by his own or other denominations. When the American Board of Commissioners of Foreign Missions commenced sending the gospel to foreign and heathen lands, Mr. Johnston brought the subject before his people, and secured their liberal and efficient aid. He did the same also in regard to the American Education Society. At one time he entertained for several days, and lodged in his garret (the spare rooms in his house being occupied by other guests), five or six Indians on their way from their homes in the wilderness to a school established for them in Cornwall, Connecticut.

In several cases missionary families, under the direction of the A. B. C. of Foreign Missions, were entertained and helped forward on their way by the liberality of his congregation.

Through the contributions of his congregation, and of individuals belonging to it, he received more than a dozen of certificates of life membership in different benevolent religious societies. By the same means his name is enrolled as a life member of all the boards in the Presbyterian church. Besides these contributions for objects of general interest, agents for colleges, academies, and churches frequently visited Newburgh, and always received more or less. If every congregation in the Presbyterian church, through the influence of its pastor, would contribute as liberally as did the congregation of Newburgh, there would be no need of agents going from place to place to stir up the people to the performance of their duty. The treasury of our boards would be full, and the demands of our growing population supplied. In connexion with contributions for domestic and foreign missions, the monthly concert of prayer was regularly observed by the church in Newburgh, believing that prayer and giving the means of sending the gospel to the destitute, should always be connected—that the one without the other was of little avail.

At home and abroad, Mr. Johnston made notes of passing events, so that from his memoranda dates of many events otherwise not to be found might be ascertained. Some of these memoranda we shall insert in the Appendix (I). Among his manuscripts we find a book of one hundred and thirty-three closely written pages containing an account of one hundred and forty ministers, with some of whom he had been connected in Presbytery. Few of them were alive at the time of his death, and the greater part of them had changed their location, some of them more than once. And every congregation in his Presbytery had changed their minister, some of them four or five times. At the time of his death, it is believed, there was no Presbyterian minister, nor, perhaps, of any denomination, in the State of

New York who had preached so long to the same people.

The minutes of the Presbytery of Dutchess, extending from 1762 to 1795, after its dissolution were providentially found and rescued from oblivion by Mr. Johnston. These records ought to be in the hands of the Historical Society of the Presbyterian Church. From these records, and from other authentic sources, Mr. Johnston has written a brief account of several ministers connected with the Presbytery of Dutchess. Vid. specimen in Appendix I.

In 1840, the subject of this notice, unexpectedly and greatly to his surprise, was elected a trustee of the college of New Jersey. He had not sought nor anticipated the honor of so responsible an office. It was amusing to hear him tell with child-like simplicity his astonishment on reading in the well known handwriting of the clerk of the Board, the announcement of this appointment. "I could not," said he, "believe my own eyes. Is it possible that I who was once a poor ploughboy, am invited to be a guardian of that venerable institution, which has educated some of the most distinguished men, whose names adorn the annals of our country?" Those who knew the man will not say that this was affected humility. It was an honest expression of what he really and truly felt. Afterwards, when he took his seat at the Board, the same feelings attended him. "I have often," said he, "looked round, and saw myself surrounded with some of the most distinguished men of the state and neighboring cities, the governor, the judges of the Supreme Court, the lawyers, the professors of the theological seminary, the ministers of the gospel: and I have covered my face, and shed tears at the thought of my unworthiness of such a seat."

As an evidence of the estimation in which he was held by the community, La Fayette College in 1848 conferred on this unassuming man, the honorary degree of Doctor in Divinity. It is not known whether he ever accepted or declined this honor. Certain it is, that he who recorded very minute occurrences in his life, has left no written notice of this event. It is believed, that this title never sat easy on him. He did not think himself possessed of those splendid talents and profound erudition which merit this high distinction. It is true, he had ordinary talents, was a good mathematician—could read Latin and Greek, was well acquainted with the teachings of the Sacred Scriptures, and studied the Westminster Confession of Faith, including the Shorter and Longer Catechisms. We have looked over several hundred pages of his manuscripts, and we are free to say, we have not noticed more than two words incorrectly spelled; and this is saying more than can be said of some brethren of the cloth, who display at the ends of their names, two large "semilunar fardels." Our friend had more substantial honors.

CHAPTER IX.

Review of his Ministry—Seven Discourses—His last illness—Noble Resolution of his Congregation—The Visit of Two Friends—Partial Recovery—Attends Commencement at Princeton—His Death—Funeral Services.

In the summer of 1854, Mr. Johnston commenced a series of lectures, which he called a review of his ministry. We do not know that he had any presentiment that his ministry was so near a close. He was in good health, and able to preach and perform all the duties of his office without exhaustion. It is probable, he thought, that as he was approaching four-score years, the end of his ministry could not be far off, and that he would look back and lead his people to look back on what was past, and forward to what would shortly come.

As the foundation of these discourses, he chose the following words:—" Unto him be glory in the church by Jesus Christ, throughout all ages, world without end. Amen!"—Ephesians iii. chap., 21st verse. He undertook to show what the church is—the different forms it has assumed under different dispensations—that God loves the church—the ways in which he has manifested his love—the future prospects of the church—its universality and final triumphs—the end for which it was instituted—the manifestation of the glory of God through Jesus Christ—that the church universal, including believers of all ages and of all nations—every particular church, and every member of that church, always had brought, and always will, in ages to come and throughout eternity, bring glory to God—that it is the duty of the church, in all its branches, and in all its members, to aim at this end—the ways in which it is to be accomplished—that it is through the preaching of the gospel, accompanied by the prayers and holy example of all who love our Lord Jesus Christ, that the church is to be collected and edified, and prepared to ascribe glory to God "throughout all ages, world without end. Amen!" With the discussion of these and similar topics, Mr. Johnston interspersed statements respecting the churches of Newburgh and New Windsor—relating what God had done for them—what they had done and what they had left undone—and what it was their duty to do in time to come. From this course of lectures chiefly we have collected the fragments of history given in the preceding pages relating to the churches of Newburgh and New Windsor, and the Presbyteries with which they were connected. It is to be regretted that these discourses are not written out in full. If they had been left in a state fit to be published they would have been an inestimable legacy to the people of his charge, and to the church at large. In this series he had delivered seven discourses, and it was in his mind to prepare and deliver two more. But his work in the pulpit was done. The last discourse was delivered on the 14th of January, 1855, and he was laid prostrate so that he did not leave his bed chamber for six weeks. He had, in December preceding, an attack of rheumatism, yet he had been able to attend a meeting of the trustees of the college at Princeton, a few days before Christmas. As soon as he was unable to appear in the pulpit, before there was any apprehension that his life was so near a close, a committee waited upon him and requested him to feel no anxiety respecting the services of the pulpit, that the congregation would have it supplied, and that his usual salary would be continued to him during life. This was a just and honorable movement—a high testimonial of his people's estimate of his character, and of their gratitude for his long and faithful services. Dr. Johnston wrote to Princeton, in a scrawling hand, scarcely legible, for a young man to fill his pulpit, and he came, and the good man's mind was at rest on that subject. Of all the maladies to which the human frame is liable, perhaps the rheumatism is the most difficult to be endured with patience. Sickness and pain was a new thing to the patient; through a long life he had enjoyed health and the power of bodily action—now to be confined to a chamber and bed of pain was a severe trial. But, whatever expressions of impatience may have escaped his lips, it is believed that his soul was at rest. His heart was stayed on God, and he remembered with gratitude the agonies of a dying Saviour. He also often expressed his gratitude for the comforts that surrounded him amidst his pains and sufferings—a sympathizing and grateful people—an affectionate wife—kind and attentive children. The writer of this tribute to the memory of a long tried friend, in company with another friend, made him a visit in the month of April, and found him in his cushioned chair—tears and not words expressed his joy. After a short interval of silence, conversation commenced, and he resumed his wonted vivacity and cheerfulness. It was Saturday afternoon; we passed the Sabbath in Newburgh, and had the pleasure of seeing our friend come down with assistance into the parlor, and we spent a pleasant and profitable day. Having expressed a strong desire to meet once more with the Trustees of the College of New Jersey, he was invited to come a week before Commencement and recruit his health. He came, accompanied by a daughter to take care of him, and although feeble, seemed to enjoy the visit. Attending the meeting of the Board of Trustees, and participating in their deliberations, was the last public duty he performed.

The day after Commencement, the 27th of June, no persuasions could induce him to remain longer. The heat and dust in the crowded cars was too much for his feeble frame; yet he reached New York, passed over to Staten Island, and spent the night in the family of a friend, and the following day returned to Newburgh. Through the month of July, there was no mitigation in his pains, and about the first of August another excruciating disease commenced, which terminated his sufferings on the twenty-third of that month. "There is one event," says Solomon, "to the righteous and to the wicked." They must both die; and they may die in the same manner as to their bodily sufferings; but there is a vast difference in the peace of the soul, in which happiness chiefly consists. There is an immeasurable difference in what follows. The one may pass from a bed of agony to a state of bliss unspeakable and full of glory. The other may go without apparent pain to unending woe. On the 26th, the funeral services were conducted with great simplicity. And he who, according to his own estimate, had presided and preached at the funerals of at least twenty-five hundred persons, was carried to his grave. Before the removal of the corpse from the house, the Rev. Dr. Brown, of the Episcopal church, read the 15th chapter of 1 Corinthians, and the Rev. Souther Peck, of the Methodist Episcopal church, offered an appropriate prayer. At two o'clock P. M., the whole population of Newburgh seemed to assemble at the church. The clergy of all the Protestant denominations in Newburgh, ministers from the surrounding country, and numerous friends from distant parts of Orange county, were there. The services were introduced by the Rev. Samuel H. McMullen, invoking the divine blessing, and reading the 90th Psalm. After the singing of an appropriate hymn, the Rev. James Scott, pastor of the Baptist church, Newburgh, offered a devout and solemn prayer, which was followed by an able and impressive sermon from the Rev. Dr. Potts, of the city of

New York, who was providentially in the place. The object of the preacher was to show the extensive and lasting influence for good or for evil which a single man may have, and often has had, on the community in which he lives, and on the world. He said only a few words respecting the deceased; but the influence which the good man exerts in life, and frequently after his body is in the grave, so well and so eloquently exhibited, the audience could not avoid applying to the brother recently departed. They thought of the reformation in morals, and of the numerous souls converted in Newburgh, of the ministers of the gospel brought forward and trained, of the scholarships established for educating others, of the funds contributed for missionary and other benevolent purposes, through the instrumentality of this one man. They looked forward to the results which may follow in distant ages from a single impulse given by a feeble arm—results which, like the waves produced by a pebble cast on the bosom of a placid lake, spread wider and wider until they reach the distant shores; that a single convert may be the means of training a pious family, and each of these another and another; that every minister transplanted from this nursery may be the means of propagating others, and they others; that the missionaries sent forth and sustained in heathen lands by the contributions of this people, may, combined with the efforts of other churches in our own and in other Christian lands, spread the truth as it is in Jesus until "the knowledge of the Lord shall cover the earth" as the waters cover the bosom of the great deep.

After the services in the church, the wide and long procession, chiefly on foot, without any formal order, followed the corpse to its resting-place. We do not know that business was stopped or shops closed by order of the municipal authority, but there was silence, and no one was seen moving as far as the eye could reach, except those in the procession. It was a beautiful serene summer afternoon, not oppressively hot. The body was deposited in a lot purchased by Mr. Edward R. Johnes, a member of the congregation, and presented to the family, in a new cemetery, delightfully situated a quarter of a mile south-west of the village, and from which there is a picturesque view of the noble Hudson and the surrounding highlands. A few fitting words were said at the grave by the Rev. Dr. McLaren, of the Reformed Dutch church, and the body was committed to the earth, there to rest until the morning of the resurrection. The solemn rites were closed by singing the Christian doxology, and by the apostolic benediction.

NOTICE.

THE accompanying Lithograph, the design of a monument about to be erected to the memory of Dr. Johnston, was handed to the Publisher after the work had been printed, and was in the hands of the binder. We have delayed the binding to have it inserted in the book. As the inscription on the monument indicates, it is another testimonial of the community in which he lived, and a lasting memorial of their kindness and veneration for his memory.

The reduced proportions of the monument, as shown in the Engraving, require the inscription on the entablature to be given in such small characters as to be illegible; we therefore repeat it below in a more distinct form.

THE PUBLISHER.

DESIGN FOR A MONUMENT
proposed to be erected
in memory of
The late Rev.[d] Dr. John Johnston.
1856.

HE WAS BORN IN MONTGOMERY N.Y. 28 JAN. 1778. GRADUATED AT THE COLLEGE OF NEW JERSEY PRINCETON IN 1801 ORDAINED AND INSTALLED PASTOR OF THE PRESBYTERIAN CHURCH IN NEWBURGH 5 AUG 1807 IN WHICH OFFICE HE DIED 23 AUGUST 1855.

THOU SHALT COME TO THY GRAVE IN A FULL AGE LIKE AS A SHOCK OF CORN COMETH IN IN HIS SEASON JOB V. 26.

THE CITIZENS OF NEWBURGH CHERISHING AN AFFECTIONATE VENERATION FOR ONE WHO FOR NEARLY HALF A CENTURY ADORNED HIS SACRED OFFICE BY HIS PURITY AND FIDELITY AND IN EVERY RELATION OF LIFE COMMANDED THE RESPECT OF ALL WHO KNEW HIM HAVE UNITED IN ERECTING THIS MONUMENT TO HIS MEMORY.

LITH. OF SARONY & C° N.Y.

CHAPTER X.

Concluding Summary.

THE general character of the deceased will be sufficiently understood from the preceding narrative. A few peculiarities seem to be worthy of a more distinct notice. In infancy and boyhood his frame was so delicate that a short life was anticipated. By walking a considerable distance to school, by working on a farm, by long journeys in Pennsylvania and Maryland, by visiting an extensive parish, and supplying vacant congregations soon after his ordination, and all on horseback, his constitution was so strengthened that he enjoyed remarkable health during a long life. The lot also on which his house stood, containing about half an acre, was partly planted with vines and fruit trees, and partly cultivated in vegetables, all worked chiefly with his own hands, afforded him exercise and profit. At the age of seventy-six he remarked that he was then probably enjoying the benefit of work done in his garden forty years before. In stature he was about the medium height, slender, and at no time inclined to corpulency. His diet was chiefly vegetables, milk and bread, abstaining through his whole life from animal food. Hence he recorded his learning to eat oysters at Amboy, returning home from college, as a remarkable event. His abstinence from animal food was not from any religious scruples, nor from a regard to health, but simply because he had no relish for it. Of intoxicating drinks, as a beverage, he made no use. Notwithstanding his spare diet, his slender frame was capable of enduring great labor. Active, wiry, elastic, when bent down by the labors of the day, it rose again erect after a night's rest. After preaching three times on Sabbath, and returning home late at night in cold weather from a weekly lecture, he was seldom hoarse, and his voice never failed. His disposition was naturally cheerful and buoyant, not subject to permanent gloom and melancholy. He had, it is true, hours of deep depression, but these arose from moral causes, and not from a morbid and diseased body, as is frequently the case with some good and pious men. When the cause was removed, he resumed his wonted cheerfulness. In social intercourse with his family and friends he took great delight. In conversation he indulged in pleasantry and a hearty laugh. He had an acute perception of the ridiculous. Hence the ready replies and spontaneous wit of the native Irish, even when at his own expense, gave him great amusement.* He had a peculiar facility of introducing conversation with strangers in such a way as not to be regarded as impertinent and obtrusive. His simple and easy address secured at once the confidence, and opened the lips of the most reserved and taciturn. In travelling in steamboats, or stages, or railroad cars, or elsewhere, he formed new acquaintances which oftentimes terminated in lasting friendships. There was a simplicity, an openness, a candor about the man,

* See Appendix K.

which disarmed suspicion and inspired confidence in what he said or did. This confidence was never abused. No man was further from finesse. He despised artifice and trick. He abhorred management and art in accomplishing even a good object. He always came out openly, and avowed the end which he wished to obtain. He was no politician in church or in state. You always knew where he was and what he was.

Another trait of character which we rejoice to say does not belong to him exclusively, was economy in managing his domestic concerns, and freedom from a sordid and worldly spirit. A man whose income is small and limited, must be economical if he wishes to avoid worldly cares and embarrassment. He began housekeeping poor, and he did not by marriage obtain a fortune; yet he fed, and clothed, and educated ten children, four sons and six daughters, on a small salary. He engaged in no speculation in houses or lands or stocks—he did not farm, nor teach, nor employ himself in mechanical arts to increase his worldly substance. He devoted his whole time to the spiritual benefit of his people; yet on a salary of less than one-third of what is usual in the City of New York, he supported his family, maintained a liberal hospitality, and contributed to various benevolent objects. It should be remembered, that in consequence of easy and daily communication the expense of the necessaries of life is nearly the same in Newburgh as in the city. In doing this, it required the concurrence and aid of his wife. Indeed, it was to her industry and economy that we are to attribute his success in avoiding embarrassment. We know not what Dr. Johnston may have said to others, but in a frequent intercourse of more than thirty years, when we spoke freely on almost every subject, the writer never heard him complain of the straitness of his circumstances, or express a fear that at his decease he would leave his family destitute; but more than once we have heard him speak of the goodness of God, and the kindness of his people towards himself and his family. And no husband or father was more affectionate or more desirous of the welfare of his wife and children. His maxim was, "do your duty and the Lord will provide."

For tenderness of conscience he was very remarkable ; so that when he had done anything amiss, or neglected his duty, he had no peace or rest until he had made humble and penitent confession. Of many cases that might be mentioned, let one suffice : On board of a steamboat, we think it was, he made the acquaintance of the Austrian Consul. The conversation turned on mineralogy, a science in which the baron (for that was his title) was greatly interested. It was agreed that they would explore the mines in the Highlands for specimens. At the time appointed, the baron called very early in the morning at the house of Dr. Johnston. The latter had not had family prayers, and he was afraid it would not be agreeable to the baron, as perhaps he was a freethinker or a bigoted Roman Catholic, and he would omit family worship. Through the whole day he was miserable. On his return home, he went to his chamber, fell on his knees, confessed his sin, and promised the Lord that if forgiven he would not do so again. The explorations were not finished, and the following morning the baron came again early ; Dr. Johnston informed him that he had not had family worship and requested him to wait until he had performed that duty. "Certainly," said the baron, "and with your permission I will be happy to join you." After prayers, the baron from politeness, or because he felt what he said, expressed great gratification. In relating the incident to a friend, Dr. Johnston added, "what a mean coward I was —a hundred times worse than Peter, for I had not the same cause to deny my Lord and Master."

On reviewing the life of this village pastor, it is obvious that in his proper sphere he had great influence, and was instrumental in doing much good. The question arises, to what did he owe this influence—what gave him the power of doing so much good? Undoubtedly it was the Lord who was pleased to crown his labors with success. But although God can, and often does produce great results by means utterly inadequate in human view, on examination we usually find that there was something in the means employed suited to accomplish the end proposed. This is a wise and benevolent appointment; if it were otherwise, we would not know what preparation to make, nor what means to use in any work which we undertake. It was not by profound erudition and abstruse logical argument that Dr. Johnston obtained his influence. It was not by splendid eloquence, beautiful and dazzling imagery and flowers of rhetoric that he enchained the attention and excited the admiration of his hearers. Much less was it by the smoothness and polish of chaste and elegant language, that he drew around him an affectionate and pious people, and retained their confidence and love for forty-eight years. Dr. Johnston understood the meaning and the force of words, and the grammatical structure of sentences, but in the pulpit and in conversation, if a homely and quaint expression would better make known his meaning, he did not hesitate to use it. The flowers of speech and the brilliant scintillations of the imagination, which draw admiring multitudes after a popular speaker, were unknown in the pulpit of the village pastor. He never stood on the platform at our religious anniversaries and delighted a crowded audience with his eloquence.

While others were eulogizing the Bible or urging the claims of domestic and foreign missions in our populous cities, he was doing the work at home—collecting funds to print and distribute the Bible—funds to send out and sustain missionaries in the domestic and foreign field—and more than that, he was training young men and young women too, to labor in the Lord's vineyard. Although he was a director in the Theological Seminary at Princeton thirty-eight years, and punctually attended the meetings of the Board, he never could be persuaded to preach the annual sermon before the directors, or to deliver the address to the students at the close of the year; but he dropped a word into the ear of Robert and Marion Hall and Gilbert King, and secured two scholarships for that institution.

The question returns: To what did he owe his influence and power to do good? In answer to this question, our first remark is, that it was to his sincere and earnest desire to glorify God through Jesus Christ. This, we are authorized from the whole tenor of his life to believe, was his aim. "Him that honoreth God will God honor."

Intimately connected with the preceding remark is another. Dr. Johnston was a man of prayer, and he encouraged and urged his people to pray. He believed in the efficacy of prayer. He felt his dependence on the blessing of God, and he believed that without his blessing no other means could be effectual in convincing and converting sinners, and in building up the kingdom of the Redeemer. The precious revival in 1843 was commenced and carried on chiefly by prayer, with very little regular and formal preaching.

Our second remark is, that he exerted a salutary and extensive influence by preaching the gospel in a plain, affectionate, and earnest manner, "not with enticing words of man's wisdom, but in demonstration of the spirit and of power." He used in the pulpit great plainness of speech. No hearer could for a moment think that he used the pulpit to display his talents, his learning, or his eloquence. Every hearer, whatever he might think of the doctrine, was compelled to believe that the preacher was in earnest, that he really believed what he taught. His words had weight, especially with those acquainted with his consistent and exemplary life.

If a man's daily walk and conversation be not as becometh the gospel, his most eloquent and solemn appeals in the pulpit will be regarded as professional declamation, and have no salutary, but rather an injurious effect. In the case before us we have a long, uniform, and consistent life, without one foul blot on his Christian character. Imperfections and defects there were, but nothing which the world or pious Christians could censure. The preaching of such a man cannot fall unheeded on the ear. In Fairfax County, Virginia, some forty years ago, there was an aged man who had been a preacher in the Methodist connexion for forty or fifty years—a man of ardent piety and exemplary Christian life. The Methodists, by way of eulogy, used to call his preaching "bacon and greens"—a dish not very tempting from its novelty and exquisite flavor, but always good, substantial, and seldom wanting, whatever else there might be on a Virginia table. Such was the preaching of this good man, plain, affectionate, solemn, exhibiting the simple truths of the gospel in such a way that the most ignorant could understand them, and calculated to quicken and edify the intelligent and devout Christian. I once had the pleasure of hearing the good old man preach. It was a plain homespun discourse, calculated to awaken impenitent sinners, and to comfort and edify pious people. If I had to make a choice, I would rather live on "bacon and greens" the year round, than on those flimsy, whipped up, frothy syllabubs, which, how luscious soever to the taste, vanish into air the moment they touch the lips.

Dr. Johnston was a prudent man. We do not mean that he had a cautious, calculating turn of mind more properly called cunning, which takes advantage of the prejudices and passions of men, in order to bring them to favor a proposed measure. His prudence was the offspring of a well meaning heart, and not of a crafty mind. He was fixed and determined in things essential, accommodating and yielding when obvious duty was not concerned. His prudence was manifested in the management of his church and congregation. His people were composed of almost all nations, and had received all kinds of early religious training. They were from Scotland, Ireland, New England, New Jersey, and natives of New York. Some had been brought up Scotch or Irish Presbyterians, some Congregationalists, some Dutch Reformed, and some were native Presbyterians; and yet their pastor so conducted that no serious schism took place among them during forty-eight years. His session also was composed of men from different places, and brought up under different forms of church government, and yet their views and actions were brought to harmonize in all essential principles, although they sometimes differed in subordinate matters. This fact he mentions with gratitude in his last discourses.

Out of the pulpit, in his daily intercourse and parochial visits, he did as much, or, perhaps, more good than by public discourses. In conversation he had a peculiar and happy talent. Always easy, simple, and natural in his address, he gained ready access to all classes of persons. From the common occurrenees of life he could pass without effort to the interests of the soul. His countenance was not always clothed in gloom and sadness, so that young persons were glad to meet him in private or in the social circle, and they seldom failed to receive benefit from the interview. To those not acquainted with the man the above delineation may appear too highly colored. But from an acquaintance of nearly three score years, and frequent intercourse and intimate friendship more than half that time, the writer, if he said anything, could not say less. Unpretending as he was, and unknown to fame, his remembrance will live in the hearts of those who know his worth, and the church will reap the fruits of his labors in ages yet to come.

If we closed our summary without adding that Dr. Johnston owed much of his influence and usefulness to that excellent woman who was the partner of his joys and his sorrows nearly half a century, we would not have told the whole truth.* Her wise and affectionate counsels aided him in doubtful and difficult cases; soothed him in his sorrows and in his joys; managed with discretion his domestic concerns; and enabled him to devote his time to the spiritual interests

* See Appendix L.

of his people. Mrs. Johnston did more than many ministers' wives can do, or ought to be expected to do. She sought out the poor and afflicted, supplied their wants, or obtained assistance from others. She visited, and nursed, and watched with the sick and the dying. So frequently had she been with the sick, and so often had she noticed the prescriptions of physicians, that the diagnosis of disease, and the remedies that ought to be applied, were as well known to her as to the medical attendant. Her eyes are now too dim ever to read these lines. And what if the twilight of her day should be cheered by the knowledge that her labors of love are remembered and appreciated? It would not, we are certain, cause her to think more highly of herself than she ought to think. It would not prevent her feeling and saying she was an unprofitable servant, and that she had done no more than she ought to have done. Her hope of eternal life, we believe, is built on a more sure foundation than anything she has done or can do.

APPENDIX.

A.

The editor of the preceding narrative, in the fall of 1803 spent two or three weeks in the adjacent counties of Westmoreland and Fayette, which lie east of Washington county in which Dr. Johnston was, and he witnessed the religious excitement affecting the body, in the same way as above described, and he can bear testimony to the correctness of the statement made. The same remark respecting the apparent coldness of the ministers who preached, occurred to the writer that Dr. Johnston makes respecting those in Washington county. I was well acquainted with the men, and had frequently heard them preach years before, and I thought their preaching was not near equal in animation and power, to that which I had often heard from the same men. They dwelt much less than formerly on the terrors of the Divine Law. They spoke chiefly of the fulness and richness of the gospel, and the suitableness of the plan of salvation to the wants of guilty and ruined sinners. And yet when the love and mercy of God through Jesus Christ was proclaimed, the outcry and falling down in the assemblies, were as frequent as when the doom of the impenitent was proclaimed. I seldom heard a sermon or conversation in which it was not fully and plainly stated that there is no religion in falling down, convulsions of the body, nor even in involuntary crying out. People were exhorted to restrain their feelings and to listen to the truths of God's Word. After these exhortations the outcry would be suspended for a few moments, and then would break out with increased violence. I conversed with both the friends and enemies of the work, and all were agreed that the falling down and bodily agitations, whatever might be the cause, were involuntary; and that those who cried out could not restrain themselves. It was wonderful how little confusion the falling and shrieking, for so it might be called, produced. Some one near the person who fell, would take care that he did not hurt himself, when his motions were violent; others would not turn their head to see what had occurred, even when attended with a loud shout. Sometimes, as stated in the narrative, individuals would lie quiet and not move a limb or a muscle, others would be convulsed in such a manner that you would think every muscle would be broken, and every joint dislocated. And yet I conversed with several who were thus affected, and they assured me that at the time they felt no pain, and afterward no soreness or stiffness in their limbs or bodies. I never learnt that any one sustained any permanent injury in body or mind, from this mental excitement, and these bodily spasms.

In Kentucky and Tennessee, where similar religious excitement commenced and prevailed some two years previous, it ran in some cases into the wildest fanaticism. A few Presbyterian ministers fell into the delusion, and went far astray in doctrine and in practice,—some eventually saw their error, sorely repented of their folly, and returned to the bosom of the church from which they had strayed. Others continued in their delusion and finally joined the Shakers, or became leaders in a religion somewhat similar. To the discrimination which the ministers of Western Pennsylvania made between what was essential to true religion and what was not, we may attribute under God the exemption of that part of the church from similar delusion and ruin. These strange occurrences present to the Christian, and to the student of human nature, a subject worthy of deep consideration. We cannot suppose there is anything miraculous in persons suddenly falling, and becoming entirely incapable of self-management, and at the same time retaining their consciousness, hearing what was said, and knowing the persons around them. From universal testimony, affectation and voluntary deception are out of the question. Any one who saw what occurred, would say at once imitation is impossible. It could not be counterfeited. It was involuntary beyond all doubt. From what cause the extraordinary phenomena arose, is a question to which various answers will probably be given. To us the following solution appears to be the most satisfactory. In all cases it is known and universally admitted that the mind has a great effect upon the body. Violent passions of any kind will agitate the whole frame. Terror will cause the limbs and muscles to tremble. Joy will cause the subject to leap and dance. So powerful are these emotions that the animal frame sometimes sinks under their pressure, and swooning and even death follow. This being the law of human nature, why should not religious excitement, either from joy or terror, prostrate the body? When Belshazzar, amidst his impious feast, saw the mysterious hand-writing upon the wall, "his countenance changed, and his thoughts troubled him, so that the joints of his loins were loosed, and his knees smote one against another." When Paul "reasoned of righteousness, temperance, and judgment to come, Felix trembled." When a sudden light shone from heaven Saul on his way to Damascus persecuting the Church "fell to the earth." Joy will also produce involuntary bodily emotions. Hence "to leap," to "clap the hands," to "shout for joy," are common expressions, all denoting that joy, without any action of the will, produces these bodily motions. It must be admitted that the truths revealed in the Bible, if fully believed, are calculated to make a deep impression on the mind, and to produce intense fears or enrapturing hopes, according as the person thinks himself concerned in the threatenings or promises announced. It is because men do not fully and practically believe they are in such a sinful state and in such imminent danger, as the Bible teaches, that they can hear without emotion the awful threatenings of the Divine Law. The same is true as respects the promises of the gospel. There is a mist—a darkness—resting on the minds of the penitent and impenitent, which obscures their vision, and causes them to view these things rather as shadows than as realities. Let their faith or belief become "the substance," the embodiment "of things hoped for," or feared, and "the evidence," the irresistible proof of "things not seen," and the effect will be great. Heaven and hell may be believed to exist, but they are viewed as afar off; let them be brought nigh as they are on a death-bed, and both the saint and the sinner cannot feel tranquil and unmoved. The displeasure of God against sin may be admitted, but its manifestation is considered as future, and the sinner hopes to repent before he dies, and his conscience is at rest; but let him feel that the unbelieving, as our Lord declares, is condemned already, and the wrath of God abideth on him at the present moment, and who can say what the effect may be on the mind, and on the body? It is not unreasonable to believe that the ministration of the Word of God which is sharper than a two-edged sword, accompanied by the influence of the Holy Spirit, may pierce the soul with such anguish as to prostrate the body, and cause the convicted sinner to call aloud for mercy.

Suppose in a general awakening, some six or eight or more persons should be brought under such deep conviction for sin as to force them to cry aloud for mercy, and fall prostrate, is it not probable that the attention of others would be excited, that they would enter into the feelings of those thus exercised, and that mysterious principle which we call sympathy would begin to work? The cheerful countenance of a friend will take the gloom from our own in moments of dejection. The tears in another's eyes will cause our tears to flow when we have no cause of sorrow, and even when we do not know why our friend weeps. The principle is universal. We cannot associate with others and not imbibe their spirit, and imitate their actions. A case in point occurs to my mind. I had under my tuition a boy of some fourteen years old. I know he did not stutter or have any impediment in his speech. His parents were absent one week, and the boy played truant and spent his time gunning and fishing in company with a man who stuttered and stammered in his speech so as to be scarcely intelligible. The boy returned to school, and he stuttered and stammered so that it was painful to hear him read or speak. On the same principle, we think it probable that persons who were under no conviction for sin, or fear of "judgment to come," might lose the command of their muscles, and fall prostrate merely by looking at others. If this principle be admitted it will confirm the truth of the declaration made by many persons during this extraordinary excitement, that they were not conscious of any anxiety on account of their sins before or at the time they fell prostrate, and unable to control the motions of their limbs. But if it be true that some were affected through sympathy, it will not prove that all were affected from the same cause. At the commencement there must have been some other cause; sympathy could not have commenced the work, for there was none in a condition to excite sympathy; and many, very many declared, that it was their deep conviction for sin, or their joy for deliverance from condemnation, that so overwhelmed them that they lost the power of voluntary motion. But suppose there was much mingled with this remarkable revival that did not belong to true religion, so there is also in revivals when there is no bodily agitation. The fruits in both cases prove that the work is of God.

B.

Mr. Johnston states, in a paper before me, that he has notices of the untimely and horrid deaths of a considerable number of those belonging to the Druid Society, but adds that these notices taken from his own observation, or from testimony that cannot be disputed, ought not to be published during the life of immediate and near relatives. These papers we have not seen, but it is a notorious fact that several belonging to the Druid Society died drunkards, committed suicide, or came to their end in a horrid manner. In the grave-yard in Newburgh, there is a stone, which after giving the name of the deceased, and the date of his death, adds, "A victim of intemperance." This stone was erected and the inscription written by an inebriate son of the deceased.

Such are the effects of infidelity—"Without natural affection."

C.

"There stood up," &c., evidently alluding to the form of admitting members to full communion in New-England Churches, and adopted by many Presbyterian Churches in the state of New York. On these occasions, those received on examination, stand up before the pulpit, and give their assent to the leading doctrines contained in the confession of faith and catechisms of the Presbyterian Church, and in some cases publicly covenant to submit to the government and discipline of the Church, when administered according to the Word of God. Mr. Johnston thought this mode of admitting members, much more solemn and impressive than that of silently receiving members to the Lord's Table after examination and approval by the session, as had been practised in the congregation before he had become pastor. It let the members of the church know those who were fellow-communicants, and it had also a solemn and salutary effect on those who were not communicants. The form may not be expressly commanded in the Sacred Scriptures, yet there is nothing in it contrary to the spirit of the gospel, which requires Christians to let the world know they are not ashamed of their Lord and Master.

"The youngest," says Mr. Johnston, "that ever I received into the church was Adelia Drake, aged nine years, three months, and twenty-three days; while she lived she adorned by an exemplary life the doctrine of God, her Saviour, and when she died, gave evidence that she had gone to be for ever with the Lord. Another was only thirteen years and twenty days old. Of him it might be said that he feared God from his youth; his attention was early turned to the gospel ministry, and he prosecuted his studies with that view. He is now (1852) a seaman's chaplain, and promises to be very useful." The oldest was Mr. Isaac Belknap in his eightieth year. The day that he came to see me and converse with me, was the 26th day of December, 1812. He had attended the funeral of General James Clinton, the day before, which was Christmas-day, and very cold. When he came into my room I was surprised and rejoiced to hear him say in answer to my question, 'How he was,' 'I am an old sinner, few and evil have been the days of the years of my pilgrimage.' He was greatly distressed, and after prayer he returned home; about four months afterwards he united with the church. He grew in grace, particularly humility, and died a most triumphant death, April 29th, 1815."

"I well remember a conversation which I had with one, who is now, I trust, in a better world. Her great distress was, that she knew little or nothing of the distresses of which she heard others speak, in view of exposure to the wrath of God. 'Well,' said I, 'if you should arrive at Heaven you will not regret that you had not been brought by the mouth of hell. If you hate sin, and love holiness, that is the grand characteristic of a Christian. It is not what precedes hatred of sin and love of holiness, but the exercise itself—hating sin and loving holiness—to which you should direct your attention.' She was comforted, and enabled to confess Christ before the world. She was useful in life, comfortable in death, and we have no doubt, happy in eternity, having, as she said, been "drawn by the cords of love."

D.

Attending the General Association of Connecticut, at Fairfield, in 1814, Mr. Johnston makes the following record: "I was lodged at the house of Mr. afterwards Dr. Humphries, in company with the Rev. Lemuel Haines and lady. Mr. Haines was a colored man, and known from his celebrated sermon on the text, "And the serpent said unto the woman, ye shall not surely die," which he delivered to his own people after the Universalist, Hosea Ballou, had endeavored to establish the doctrine of universal salvation. Mr. Haines was a very companionable man, a good scholar, a great wit, and very popular preacher. He was very ready to give his opinion on any subject proposed. He, like myself, was a delegate to the Association. We differed in other respects. I was a white man, and had no wife present; he was a black man, and had a white woman for his wife. We were all pleasantly and happily situated under the hospitable roof of Dr. Humphries. The business of the Association was harmoniously conducted under the moderatorship of Dr. Goodrich of Berlin. Among those who attended the Association, was Dr. Dwight, President of Yale College. Public worship was frequently performed; in short, there was an unusual number of religious exercises mingled with the ordinary business of the Association. Near the middle of the morning sessions the house was filled with spectators, and it became known that Mr. Haines was to preach. He took his seat in the pulpit between the Moderator and Dr. Dwight. His text was, 'Ho, every one that thirsteth, come ye to the waters.' It was readily perceived that the preacher had the attention of all present, especially of Dr. Dwight. And when Mr. Haines illustrated thirsting, by the case of the Syro-Phœnician woman saying 'Truth, Lord, yet the dogs may eat the crumbs that fall from their master's table,' Dr. Dwight wept like a child, and there was scarcely a dry eye in the house. The impression made on my mind was that he was a powerful preacher. He had several revivals among his own people and in neighboring congregations. His own wife was one of his spiritual children."

On his way to the General Association of New Hampshire, in 1826, he lodged with Dr. Wisner, in Boston. "In the evening a bell rang. I learned," writes Mr. Johnston, "that Dr. Palfrey, lately returned from Europe, was going to preach. Dr. Wisner declined going, but urged me to go. Dr. Palfrey took for his text, 'Ye must be born again.' In his view the text had no application to any in a gospel-enlightened land. It wholly regarded exchanging heathenism and Judaism for Christianity. He treated with pity or scorn what is usually understood by the new birth or regeneration as held by Calvinists."

E.

"The Rev. Dr. John Brown came to Newburgh the 1st January, 1816. He was the first and only rector of the Episcopal Church in Newburgh.* That church commenced, and grew up under him. The 1st of January, 1855, he had been pastor thirty-nine years."

The Rev. Joseph McCarroll became pastor of the Associate Reformed Church, the 14th day of March, 1823, so that on the 1st of January, 1855, he was pastor of the same church nearly thirty-two years. Respecting these two gentlemen and himself, Dr. Johnston remarks that "it seldom occurs in any village that three ministers of different deno-

* This remark respecting Dr. Brown commencing the Episcopal Church in Newburgh, must be understood in a qualified sense. There had been an Episcopal Church in Newburgh, at an early period, and regular worship was continued until the American Revolution. From that time until Dr. Brown commenced his ministry, there was no regular Episcopal service or organized church in Newburgh; so that the Episcopal Church may be said to have commenced and to have grown up under him.—[See Mr. Eager's Annals of Orange County.—Editor.]

minations continue to labor thirty-two years side by side, witnessing the growth of each other's charge, with a harmny of feeling, and a unity which have enabled them to rejoice that the work of the Lord was prospering, through their instrumentality. This has been the case with Drs. Brown, McCarrol, and myself; we began our ministry in our present charge, and have remained in our lot to the present time, so that each can say, 'I dwell among my own people.'"

F.

"Mr. Uzal Knapp was received a member of this church, April 5th, 1816, from a Congregational Church in Stamford, Connecticut. He still lives, and claims to be the last of Washington's Body Guards. He is about ninety-five years old, and has the use of his faculties of body and mind, except that his hearing is somewhat impaired—he still travels about, and it is not long since I saw him driving a team on the turnpike. He converses like a pious man, and next to his Saviour, he loves to talk of Gen. Washington, and fight over again the battles fought under his command. (1852.)"

Henry Tise, now gone to be with the Lord. His parents came from Germany before the middle of the last century. They understood no language but the German, and of course this was their family language; they were pious people, and Henry learned to repeat his prayers in German as he kneeled at his mother's knee. As the children grew up they mingled with English people, went to English school, and the younger part of the Tise family could not be distinguished from English. Henry married and had a numerous family. He made a profession of religion, and became an elder in the Church of Hopewell. In 1816 he removed to Newburgh, and was chosen an elder in the Presbyterian Church. He was a good man, was in the habit of visiting and praying with the sick and afflicted. He had ceased to speak the German language or to read the German Bible for years. He lived to be an old man, and was under the care of a pious daughter in his last sickness. "He gradually sank under the infirmities of age and disease. He manifested confidence in his Saviour, and had the consolations of religion as long as he was able to make known his feelings. He lay some days apparently unconscious of what was passing around him. On the morning of the day on which he died, about daylight, his daughter was awaked by him praying, and to her surprise he was praying in German, using the words his mother had taught him, four-score years before. Early impressions are lasting. From such facts parents and teachers should learn a lesson. He died, February 15th, 1845, aged 85 years, 8 months, and 21 days."

"Mr. Isaac Chaffin died on the 29th of May, 1830, in this village. His history is calculated to arrest the attention of all acquainted with it. The following details are as he communicated them to me:—

"He was a native of Jamaica, Wyndham County, Vermont. He was a rude, ungovernable youth, though he had received a pious education, and had witnessed a holy example in the life of his mother. He became infidel in his sentiment, reckless in business, extravagant in his expenses, involved his friends in pecuniary embarrassment, and ran away. He went to Louisville and Cincinnati, united with a club of Infidels and Universalists, read deistical books, ridiculed the Bible, laughed at the idea of Christ's divinity, and said he had more than once uttered the blasphemous expression, that he would as soon trust to the blood of a hog as to that of Jesus Christ, and that his conscience would check him every time he uttered the horrid sentence. His account of the club of Deists, Universalists, and Atheists in Louisville and Cincinnati, was shocking. He retained his infidel sentiments until he returned to Newburgh in 1829. His health was declining, and it was evident his days were drawing to a close. When confined to his room, he was attended by a person who brought to him his daily meals. A little toy cup containing something for him to eat, was undesignedly taken to his room. On this cup his eyes met the solemn warning, 'Prepare to meet thy God.' The thought struck him, 'There is a God, and I must meet him.' He tried to quiet his conscience, but every day the little cup came, and silently said, 'Prepare to meet thy God;' his mother rose in remembrance, her example and counsel were vividly before him, he was miserable; his infidelity fled, and he turned to the Bible for relief, pious people visited him, gave him counsel, and prayed with him, he became hopefully a new man, and he manifested the great change by sundry letters to his infidel acquaintances, warning them of their errors and danger, and exhorting them to flee to that Jesus, whom they, with him, had ridiculed. He wrote to his father and sister, asking their forgiveness, and sending messages to such as he had ill-used. This change was some time in the winter, and he lived until the latter part of May. His wish that he might live to make a public profession of religion was gratified; our communion season was the second Sabbath in May, and on that day he was carried to the Church, pale, emaciated, and in the presence of the congregation he was baptized, and received the emblems of the broken body and shed blood of the Redeemer. At the close of the service he expressed himself thus, 'God be praised, I feel thankful that my prayers have been answered; so that I was enabled to be brought to the church.' A few days after his interment, his sister came from Vermont, and confirmed the sad history which her brother had given of himself, and added that he had been shot in a duel, and the probability was that the ball was now with him in his grave, as it had not been extracted. We hope that the blood which he had once and again undervalued and contemned was applied to the washing away of his deep-dyed sins."

"William Belknap was received into the church May 8th, 1820. The time of his death I don't know, but this I do know, that he was a conscientious, good man, subject to great depression of spirits, approaching at times hypochondria. He frequently came to consult me in reference to the great adversary troubling him in bed—crawling over him, removing the clothes, shaking the bedstead, &c. I was perplexed to know what to say to him. I recommended prayer, meditation, sitting up late, and rising early, so that he would be disposed to sleep sound while in bed. The good old man followed my directions, but all would not do: the devil would still return and repeat the disturbance. At last, believing it was a mental delusion, I recommended him to take the Bible into bed with him, and when the devil came to present him with the Bible or to throw it at him. He did so, and the next day he came with a pleasant countenance, and told me he had a quiet and refreshing night's rest."

"Mary Gardner was received into the church, August 11th, 1850. She was a mute, deaf and dumb. None of the Session understood the language of signs by which mutes are enabled to communicate with each other. Through a person who understood signs, we obtained her answers to questions proposed by us. We had the testimony of her parents and neighbors, and we thought we could understand the train of thoughts passing in her mind, by the expression of her countenance. And from the whole we were satisfied to receive her to the fellowship and communion of the church. She was an attendant on public worship for several years—she seemed to enjoy religion, and she left us and went to heaven, where the organs of hearing and speaking are not necessary to communion with God."

G.

This widow lady resided about five miles above the place where Mr. Johnston crossed the river, at the margin of a forest of twelve miles, through which he had to pass. She was alone, her sons were out preparing a raft of boards for the Philadelphia market. He told her who he was and the business in which he was engaged, and asked for a night's lodging. He was directed to a field where his horse would find pasture. While he was putting his horse into the pasture the good lady had prepared for him something to eat, and when the culinary process was done, she sat down at her spinning-wheel. "I attempted," says Mr. J., "to introduce religious conversation, but the more I talked the faster the wheel went, until I could not be heard, and I had to stop—I seized the next interval, when the wheel slacked a little, and again I threw in a word, and again the wheel went whiz, whiz, whiz. I made the third attempt and the wheel went slower and slower, and at last stopped, and the good old lady covered her face with her hands, and burst into tears; when she recovered a little she said, 'I was brought up in Connecticut, was a member of the church, and left in the midst of a revival, came to this place seven years ago, lost my husband, and have not heard a sermon, nor had a person to speak to me on the subject of religion, since I came here.' Her tears fell in abundance, and we had a delightful season of prayer and Christian conversation. I have often thought of Mrs. Tyler, and I hope she is now (1852) in heaven. I have sometimes thought that her situation might be illustrated by a hickory coal having rolled from a burning fire; when it fell it was all alive, left to itself it became covered up with its own ashes; blowing away the ashes, the living spark would appear, ready to unite with another coal that might be brought in contact. The Christian, in company with others, is alive and vigorous; but if he be left alone, in the midst of the world, without any one with whom he can communicate, he will be likely to become buried up in the world; but brought into connexion with Christian friends, the grace of God in the heart will show itself, and he will be made to rejoice. "This interview," continues Mr. Johnston, "and others of a similar kind, remind me of a homely but apt comparison made at my house, by a missionary, returning from the new settlements—"*You might as well,*" said he, "*attempt to draw a cat to you by the tail, as to induce the people with whom I have been to enter into religious conversation.*"

H.

"Shortly after I entered the ministry, I was sent by the Presbytery to preach where the village of Bethel now is in the county of Sullivan. I fulfilled my appointment, and returned home, somewhat dispirited. A few weeks after a stranger came to see me, who stated that he had travelled that Sabbath morning ten miles through the woods to attend public worship, and that my sermon had produced such a state of mind that he had no peace nor rest, and that he had come to converse with me on the subject. We were both greatly affected. He remained two or three days, and then left me. I often thought of him, but gradually I lost sight of him. Years passed away, till one day, a stranger called and asked whether I knew him. I answered no, and he made himself known. Having obtained a hope of pardon, his heart was fixed on the ministry. He wandered to the West, and in the State of Indiana he commenced teaching a school, and then edited a political paper, and supported himself while prosecuting his studies. He was licensed to preach, and became a most useful and influential minister, and his name is connected with the benevolent operations of the day. At a meeting of the General Assembly in Philadelphia, a gentleman from the West informed me that he had it in charge to present to me the kind remembrances of the Rev. Thomas Lippincot. My heart was glad."

"Mr. Hopkins. When on my way to attend the General Association of New Hampshire, in 1826, I lodged from Saturday night till Monday in the house of a friend, in Salem, Massachusetts. I was urged to attend a meeting for prayer in the evening; I wished to be excused, but was almost compelled to go. And I was called upon to make some remarks, which I did from the pointed passage, 'The Master is come and calleth for thee.' I went on my way, and, shortly after I returned home, I received a letter from a Mr. Hopkins, letting me know that he had come three miles to attend the meeting, and there, for the first time, heard the gospel calling to repentance, and faith in Christ,* thanking me for the sermon and asking to be remembered in my prayers, and requesting me to make his house my home, if I again visited that part of the country. I learned from those who knew him, that he still continued to manifest the character and conduct of a Christian.

"Two or three years ago I met in a friend's house in Newburgh, a gentleman, who reached out his hand to me, and with a smiling countenance, and a tear falling over his cheek, asked, 'do you know me?' 'No.' 'Do you recollect preaching at a certain house, north of Monticello?' 'Yes,' and gave the reason why I recollected it, although it was more than thirty years before. 'Do you recollect the text?' I replied I did not. 'Well,' said he, 'I do, it was, "Unto you I call, and my voice is to the sons of men." 'That,' said he, 'was the first time that preaching had any effect on me. I hope I became a new man, I settled down in life, united with a church in Connecticut, and have been deacon in the church for nearly thirty years.' We wept and talked, and prayed together, and separated. Whether he is alive at this time, I know not. If dead, I rejoice to think he is in Heaven."

* Probably his minister, like Dr. Emmons, thought exhortations to look to Christ for repentance and faith not required, as these were blessings not procured through Christ.—Editor.

"While attending the General Assembly in Pittsburgh, one evening after public worship, a young man, whom I did not recognise, accosted me by name, saying he was once a member of our Sabbath School, and that the address I gave on the last Sabbath he was in the school was blessed to his awakening to a sense of his situation as a sinner, and he hoped he had accepted Jesus Christ as his Saviour. He united with the church, was employed in a large foundry in Alleghany City, and hoped was daily in the exercise and enjoyment of religion.

"These," adds Mr. Johnston, "are only specimens of what might be given, and show how censurable it is to conclude that no good has been done, because we do not see immediate beneficial effects."

I.

Congregations taken under the care of the North River Presbytery:—

Poundridge, May 7, 1822; originally under the care of Dutchess Presbytery; *Poughkeepsie*, September 19, 1821; *Smithfield*, April 27, 1825; *North Salem*, September 18, 1825; *South East*, April, 1825; *Cold Spring*, April, 1826; *Canterbury*, October, 1826; *Freedom Plains*, April, 1828; *Highland Congregation*, October, 1830; *Matteawan*, Dec., 1832; *Beekmanville*, September 27, 1833; *Tabernacle Church, N. Y.*, April, 1834; dissolved by Synod, October 25, 1834; *2nd Church, Poughkeepsie*, June, 1835; *Pleasant Plains*, September, 1837.

Among the biographical notices recorded by Mr. Johnston, we find the names of several that had been connected with the Presbytery of Dutchess. Among them is the following notice of one of the founders of that Presbytery:—

"The Rev. Elisha Kent was born in Suffield, Connecticut; he was graduated in Yale College, in 1729, and has A.M. attached to his name, probably from the same. He was licensed to preach by some Association in Connecticut, and ordained and installed pastor in Newtown, Ct. He is represented to have been a zealous and successful laborer in the vineyard of his Lord and Master. He was among those active ministers (in the days of Edwards, Tennant, and Whitefield) who objected to being taxed to support ministers whose labors were not approved, or, in other words, to support the established religion, as then found in Connecticut. The result was, that he and several of his people removed to the County of Dutchess, in the State of New York, and he became the pastor of the first church in Philippi, or, as now called, South East. His removal was in the year 1740, and as he said, 'to be removed from lords spiritual.' From the records of several Church Sessions we find him engaged in organizing churches and settling difficulties. In one the date is 1748, and in another 1759. Part of his time was employed in preaching to the people of the Hollow, or, as it is now called, Washington Hollow, in 1745. In 1763, he and Solomon Mead and Joseph Peck united and formed the Presbytery of Dutchess, adopting the Confession of Faith, the Larger and Shorter Catechisms, and form of Presbyterian Church Government, and as a Presbytery were received as a constituent member of the Synod of New York and Philadelphia. This was the first Presbytery ever formed north of the city of New York. The Presbytery was called 'the Presbytery of the County of Dutchess,' and afterwards changed by order of Synod to 'the Presbytery of Dutchess.' He died in 1776. He was pastor of the Church of South East about thirty-six years, and had been a preacher, and probably a pastor, in Newtown, Ct., and South East, N.Y., more than forty-four years. His name is found in the records of the Presbytery and of the Synod, as being appointed to some of the most important and difficult duties in either. He was a diligent, useful, and successful minister, and his works do follow him. His whole ministry preceded the declaration of American Independence. The late Chancellor James Kent was his grandson."

[We do not know how many children the Rev. Elisha Kent had. One daughter we happen to know, married a Mr. Kane, who lived and died in Schenectady, N.Y. She was a remarkably intelligent and pious lady, far advanced in years, when we became acquainted with her. She had five or six sons, all active and enterprising men. From these are descended many families of the name of Kane in the United States. Of that stock was the late Hon. Elias Kane, United States Senator from Illinois; the Hon. Judge Kane, of Philadelphia, and his son, Dr. Elisha Kent Kane, the intrepid explorer of the Arctic Seas, as the name of the latter indicates, are of that family. The descendants in the female line are also numerous; and devoted piety, as well as energy of character, is found in the blood of the third and fourth generation from the Rev. Elisha Kent of "South East." A daughter of Mrs. Kane of Schenectady, a lady of distinguished piety, married a Mr. Livingston of Dutchess County, N.Y., and was the mother of the late Rev. Dr. Livingston of the Reformed Dutch Church, Philadelphia. Another daughter of the same Mrs. Kane, a lady not excelled in elegance of manners, benevolence, and piety, by any of her sex, married Jeremiah Von Rennselaer, late of Utica, and was the mother of three daughters, not inferior to herself in piety, benevolence, and refinement of manners. Two of them married distinguished gentlemen in the western part of New York, and both these, with their honored mother, sleep in Jesus. The third is single, and has charge of her sisters' children. It would be interesting, did our knowledge permit us, to trace all the branches which have sprung from the original stock—the Rev. *Elisha Kent*,—the leading founder of the Presbyterian Church, between the cities of New York and Albany.—Ed.]

K.

Mr. Johnston used with great good humor to relate several Irish anecdotes. The following, bearing hard on himself, are a specimen:—

"I had," said he, "employed an Irishman to repair a drain leading from my kitchen to the street. Having finished the drain, he was laying down the flagging that covered it. His plan did not please me, and I manifested dissatisfaction, and fretted not a little. He stopped his work, and looking at me, said, 'Mr. Johnston, there are just two things about which a man should never fret. The one is, what he can help, and the other is, what he cannot help. If he can help it, he had better go and do it; and if he cannot help it, what is the use of fretting about it?' I felt reproved," says Mr. Johnston, "and have many times had need of the same reproof."

"On another occasion," Mr. Johnston used to say, "I was looking at several laboring men engaged in removing a pile of stones. Trees had grown up among them, and the roots of the trees were interlocked with the stones, so as to make it difficult to remove the stones. One of the laborers, apparently an uncultivated, rough, ignorant Irishman, was swearing at the roots the of trees, and again and again repeating the name of the devil. I gently reproved him for doing so, and immediately he set his pick on one end, and looking very quizzically in my face, with a half triumphant smile, he said in a real Irish brogue, 'Oh, indeed, sir, I did not think you were after watching me; isn't it hard now, that because I repate the name of the ould fellow, I must be called to an account for it, and you and the like of ye are paid by the year for abusing the ould fellow?' I thought that where that shot came from there was more in store, and remembering that 'discretion is the better part of valor,' I retreated."

L.

Mrs. Johnston is a lineal descendant of the first white woman who came to reside where the village of Goshen now is, and the first who was married in Orange County. She was a woman of small stature, but of great energy and indomitable courage. Samuel W. Eager, Esq., of Newburgh, has given an interesting, and if it were proper to apply the term to authentic history, we would add, romantic account of that remarkable woman: for in respect to wild, and perilous, and daring adventure, her biography has all the elements of romance. Yet the account is a record of uncontradicted tradition in the County of Orange. When only sixteen years old, she came, without a female companion, to reside in a wilderness occupied with savages and ferocious beasts, where there was not another white woman within twenty miles of her. Her maiden name was Sarah Wells, and she married William Bull, by whom she had twelve children, all of whom lived to marry and have children. She died in 1796, aged one hundred and two years and fifteen days. At the time of her death, her descendants were:—

12 children.
98 grand-children.
212 great-grand-children.
13 great-great-grand-children.

Total, 335

The increase from these 335 descendants in sixty years which have elapsed since her death must be very great. It may be questioned, Mr. Eager remarks, if there is a family in the State that exceeds that of Sarah Bull in the number of its descendants. For a knowledge of the circumstances which led this woman to reside in an unbroken forest, amidst Indians and wild beasts, and also of the perils and labors which she underwent, we refer the reader to Mr. Eager's History of Orange County, pages 454–484.—Editor.

After the preceding pages were in the press, a journal, kept by Dr. Johnston during an excursion to the Falls of Niagara, in the summer of 1834, came into the hand of the Editor. This is believed to be the only excursion of any extent, merely for the purpose of recreation and pleasure, which Dr. Johnston took during the long period of his ministry. It occurred in this way. Mr. Thomas Powell, late of Newburgh, kindly invited Dr. and Mrs. Johnston to accompany him and his family in a tour to the Falls of Niagara, Saratoga, and intervening places, generously offering to pay the whole expense. The party consisted of Mr. and Mrs. Powell and daughter, Mr. and Mrs. Johnston, and Mr. Powell's servant, and on the way they fell in company with Mr. Ramsdell, who afterwards became the husband of Miss Powell. The journal contains interesting sketches of places visited, and incidents of travel, evincing that Mr. Johnston was an acute observer of what passed under his notice, and that he received exquisite pleasure from viewing the beautiful and sublime works of creation, and the productions of human skill and industry. Had this journal come into the hands of the Editor sooner, copious extracts would have been made, exhibiting in a favorable light the social and religious character of the Author. Amidst the delight of seeing new objects, and associating with new acquaintances, he never forgot that he was a Christian and a minister of the gospel, and he was ready on all suitable occasions to recommend the religion which he professed, and the Saviour whom he loved.

THE END.

www.ingramcontent.com/pod-product-compliance
Lightning Source LLC
LaVergne TN
LVHW012327100826
845148LV00017B/388

* 9 7 8 1 4 2 5 5 2 0 5 7 1 *